Careers in International Law

SECOND EDITION

EDITORS

MARK W. JANIS
UNIVERSITY OF CONNECTICUT SCHOOL OF LAW

SALLI A. SWARTZ
PHILLIPS GIRAUD NAUD & SWARTZ ◄•••••••••

 SECTION OF INTERNATIONAL LAW AND PRACTICE
AMERICAN BAR ASSOCIATION

Defending Liberty
Pursuing Justice

Cover design by Catherine Zaccarine

05 04 03 02 01 5 4 3 2 1

Library of Congress Cataloging-in-Publication Data

Careers in international law/[edited by] Mark W. Janis, Salli Swartz.—2d ed.
    p. cm.
    Includes index
    ISBN 1-57073-894-7
    1. International law—Study and teaching. 2. International law—Vocational
guidance—United States. 3. Lawyers, Foreign—Vocational guidance—United States.
I. Janis, Mark W. II. Swartz, Salli.

KZ1238.U55 C37 2001
341'.023'73—dc21   2001022158

Discounts are available for books ordered in bulk. Special consideration is given to state bars, CLE programs, and other bar-related organizations. Inquire at Book Publishing, ABA Publishing, American Bar Association, 750 North Lake Shore Drive, Chicago, Illinois 60611.

www.ababooks.org

Contents

Preface
by Salli A. Swartz

It is with great pleasure that Mark W. Janis and I, on behalf of the Section of International Law and Practice of the American Bar Association, present the second edition of *Careers in International Law*.

Career opportunities in international law have vastly expanded since the first edition of this book in 1993. As an indication of the changing topography of international law professions, two of the contributing authors from the first edition have changed careers within the international arena and detail their new paths in this edition. In addition, this volume includes careers that were only in the embryonic stage at the time of the first edition.

Our new authors present a refreshing outlook on the wide-ranging possibilities open to today's law students eager to practice international law. Jeffrey M. Aresty and Andrew S. Breines explain the influence of the Internet on practicing law in a small firm. Carole Silver provides an overview of the global expansion of law firms. Daryl Mundis shares his insights on practicing international criminal law, a career that hardly existed when the first edition of this book was published, and Louis Maresca describes the work of an international humanitarian lawyer, another career possibility that has greatly expanded in recent years. Clifford Hendel and I depict the practice of international law in Madrid and Paris firms, and two in-house practitioners, Carolyn Herzog and Steven Glick, share with our readers their careers with companies that do business internationally. Eleanor Roberts Lewis portrays her life in government service and Mark W. Janis contributes his views on life in academia. Marc Goldstein shares with us his career as an international commercial arbitration attorney, while John Cogan, Michael Marks Cohen, Andrew J. Markus, Daniel Magraw, and Nancy Israel have all taken the time and made the effort to update their essays from the first edition. A new appendix in this second edition features Internet resources for job seekers in international law.

It has not only been great fun recruiting the authors and editing their essays for this new edition, it also has been a true learning experience reading about the vast diversity of careers in both private and public international law. We sincerely hope that the testimonials in this edition will inspire all of our readers to pursue satisfying careers in international law.

Mark Janis and I would like to extend special thanks to our authors for sharing their insights and advice and to Beth Foxwell, publications director of the ABA Section of International Law and Practice, without whom this edition would never have existed. She was our den mother and editor-in-chief, and this book reflects her hard work and dedication.

About the Editors

Mark W. Janis is William F. Starr Professor of Law at the University of Connecticut and Sometime Reader in Law and Fellow of Exeter College, University of Oxford, England.

Salli A. Swartz is a partner at Phillips Giraud Naud & Swartz in Paris, France, and deputy editor of the ABA Section of International Law and Practice's *International Law News*.

About the Contributors

Jeffrey M. Aresty is the founder and a principal of Aresty International Law Offices, P.C. and co-editor of *The ABA Guide to International Business Negotiations, 2d ed.* Aresty is the president of LexUniversal.com, a virtual global network of independent law firms in 40 countries.

Andrew S. Breines is a principal and chief operating officer of Aresty International Law Offices, P.C. Breines is a former director of the New England Taiwan Business Council.

John P. Cogan, Jr., is an international corporate partner in the Houston office of King & Spalding, where he focuses his practice on international energy and financial and commercial transactions. He has authored numerous publications and serves as corresponding editor of *International Legal Materials*, published by the American Society of International Law.

Michael Marks Cohen is senior partner, Burlingham Underwood L.L.P., New York. He teaches the admiralty law course at Columbia Law School and is a member of the American Law Institute.

Steven M. Glick is senior vice president Business Affairs and general counsel of Paramount Home Entertainment International, a global leader in the distribution of filmed entertainment on videocassette and DVD. Glick spent the first eight years of his career in the New York, London, and Paris offices of Shearman & Sterling. Before joining Paramount in 1999, he served as director of business and legal affairs for Graseby plc (1992-1997) and as general counsel of Ladbroke Group plc (now known as Hilton Group plc) (1997-1999).

Marc J. Goldstein of Proskauer Rose L.L.P. in New York is co-chair of the International Commercial Arbitration Committee of the ABA Section of International Law and Practice and a Fellow of the Chartered Institute of Arbitrators. He devotes most of his time to international arbitration and international litigation and has published several articles on those topics.

Clifford J. Hendel is a partner at Araoz & Rueda in Madrid, where he has practiced since 1997. Previously with White & Case in New York and Paris, he spent a year between such postings as visiting foreign lawyer with Gómez-Acebo & Pompo in Madrid.

Carolyn B. Herzog is senior corporate counsel for Symantec Corporation, formerly the acting general counsel of AXENT Technologies, Inc., prior to its acquisition by Symantec. She is a resident of Washington, D.C., and focuses her practice on international intellectual property issues and technology transactions. Herzog is the co-chair of the Women's Interest Network (WIN), a committee that provides a forum within which members of the ABA Section of International Law and Practice can identify and discuss substantive issues of special interest to women involved in the practice of international law.

Nancy D. Israel practices law with Erickson Schaffer Peterson Israel & Silberman, P.C. in Wellesley, Massachusetts. Israel counsels clients on a variety of domestic and international business matters from start-up through expansion and exit. Her more specialized expertise includes foreign business arrangements, computer systems integration contracts, assessments of insurers' risks and insurance vehicles, general counsel services, and complex commercial negotiations.

Mark W. Janis is William F. Starr Professor of Law at the University of Connecticut and Sometime Reader in Law and Fellow of Exeter College, University of Oxford, England.

Eleanor Roberts Lewis is chief counsel for International Commerce at the U.S. Department of Commerce in Washington, D.C. Lewis acts as the U.S. Government Liaison for International Trade Law to the Section of International Law and Practice of the ABA.

Daniel B. Magraw is director of the International Environmental Law Office at the U.S. Environmental Protection Agency. From 1983 to 1992, he was professor of international law at the University of Colorado, where he taught public international law, international environmental law, international business transactions, and international development policy and the law. He was a visiting scientist during 1989-1990 at the Environmental and Societal Impacts Group of the National Center for Atmospheric Research, in Boulder, Colorado.

Louis Maresca is a legal adviser in the Mines-Arms Unit of the Legal Division of the International Committee of the Red Cross in Geneva, Switzerland.

Andrew J. Markus is a member of the Latin-American Practice Group of Hughes Hubbard & Reed L.L.P. in its Miami, Florida, office, and serves as General Division chair of ABA's Section of International Law and Practice.

Daryl A. Mundis is a legal officer with the Office of the Prosecutor at the International Criminal Tribunal for the former Yugoslavia and is vice-chair of the ABA International Courts Committee. He may be contacted at thehague@wanadoo.nl.

Carole Silver is senior lecturer at Northwestern University School of Law and co-director of the Certificate Program in Law & Social Science of Northwestern University and the American Bar Foundation.

Salli A. Swartz is a partner at Phillips Giraud Naud & Swartz in Paris, France, and deputy editor of the ABA Section of International Law and Practice's *International Law News.* She has practiced international business law for more than 22 years in Paris and represents numerous multinational companies concerning their European business activities as well as French companies doing business abroad.

Profile of the ABA Section of International Law and Practice

The Section of International Law and Practice is one of 24 sections within the American Bar Association and has 14,000 members worldwide. The purpose of the section is to provide information to its members and others on a variety of international legal issues. With the growing number of transactions crossing national borders, lawyers are increasingly encountering issues involving both public and private international law. To address these issues, the section has assigned 60 committees within five divisions— Business Transactions and Disputes, Business Regulation, Comparative Law, Public International Law, and General—to closely monitor and disseminate information on domestic and international policy developments with implications for law practice.

Section members can participate in any of the committees and task forces that annually produce intensive educational programs, ABA policy recommendations, and publications that can help advance their careers and serve the legal profession and the public. To cultivate discussion, the section provides its members with various list serves, Webboard conferences, and Web site pages. In addition, members receive *The International Lawyer*, the quarterly law journal on international practice; *International Law News*, a quarterly publication with updates on international practice and news regarding the section; and discounts on practical publications and programs that meet their CLE requirements.

Furthermore, the section has established several programs to advance the rule of law in the world and respond to requests for technical legal assistance. For instance, the ABA/UNDP Legal Resource Unit (LRU) assists UNDP country offices to recruit pro bono legal experts to work on governance and legal projects worldwide. These selected volunteers help reform legal systems, support electoral bodies, strengthen anti-corruption measures, and much more. The International Legal Exchange Program (ILEX) arranges an annual outbound briefing trip for legal professionals who are interested in exchanging ideas with other countries. In addition,

ILEX arranges meetings for prominent foreign lawyers, judges, and scholars with legal professionals in the United States and assists foreign lawyers who have received an offer of short-term training by a U.S. law firm to obtain J-1 visas.

Members of the section are lawyers in private practice, corporate counsel, government lawyers, professors of comparative and international law, human rights activists, law students, and LL.M. candidates. Non-U.S. lawyers also can participate in the section by becoming Foreign Associates of the ABA and joining the section. To join the Section of International Law and Practice or to learn more about the section, please visit <www.abanet.org/intlaw> or contact the ABA Service Center at 1-800-285-2221.

The American Bar Association is the largest voluntary professional membership association in the world. With more than 400,000 members, the ABA provides law school accreditation, continuing legal education, information about the law, programs to assist lawyers and judges in their work, and initiatives to improve the legal system for the public.

Lawyers on Foreign Ground

1

by Carole Silver[1]

A. INTRODUCTION

I first became interested in foreign lawyers—those lawyers whose practice is situated outside of their home jurisdictions—when I lived in Singapore in the mid-1980s while my husband was managing the Singapore office of a large U.S. law firm. I was fascinated with the ease of his transition from a several-hundred-lawyer office in the United States to a less-than-five-person office in Singapore, as well as with the differences in the nature of the practices in the two locations. His practice in Singapore was both more general and more specialized than it was in the United States. Nevertheless, the basic large law firm approach was highly valued on both sides of the globe.

Many more U.S. lawyers are working outside of the United States at the beginning of the 21st century than before.[2] This increase is directly related to the importance of international activities to the contemporary identity of nearly every elite U.S. law firm. It is insufficient today for the biggest law firms to be national only; they also must have

---

1. Many thanks to John O'Hare for insightful comments on an earlier draft, and to Franklin Morean (Northwestern LL.M. 2000) for excellent research assistance.

2. Carole Silver, *Globalization and the U.S. Market in Legal Services—Shifting Identities*, 31 LAW & POL'Y INT'L BUS. 1093, 1108-29 (2000) (chronicling the foreign office activities of the largest and most international U.S. law firms).

an international reach.[3] Foreign offices help U.S. law firms achieve this international image, and they are the sites of much of the international practice accomplished by the firms. Foreign offices serve as clear evidence of a law firm's participation in the international legal market.

U.S. lawyers are playing an increasing role in international transactions, just as international financial transactions are playing an increasing and critical role in the world economy. U.S. lawyers advise on transactions in which U.S. businesses are involved, and also on deals in which no U.S. business is involved but U.S. law nevertheless governs—a common practice in financial transactions. They also advise on certain types of transactions, such as hostile tender offers, in which U.S. expertise provides tactical value.

Changes in the global economy, including both the growing connectedness of national economies and financial markets and the increasingly important role of international financial markets, have expanded the role of law and lawyers. The new global economy favors capital markets and private financing of businesses and public projects alike. Large projects that once were funded by governments now are privatized, which creates increased roles for financial service advisers, bankers, and lawyers. The increasing internationalization of national financial markets has resulted in a growing number of foreign corporations with connections to the U.S. capital markets and a similar growth in the foreign investment opportunities available to U.S. individual and institutional investors. U.S. institutions, including securities exchanges, investment banks, and commercial lenders, participate in financial transactions around the world. They bring with them a preference for U.S. law and lawyers, which has supported the international expansion of U.S. law firms.

This expanding role for U.S. law and lawyers has coincided with two changes in the activities of participants in the international legal market. First, the largest U.S. law firms have substantially increased their penetration of the foreign market.[4] Both the absolute number of foreign offices and the average size of these offices are increasing. Second, large U.S. firms are utilizing more foreign resources. Foreign-educated and -licensed lawyers are being hired in increasing numbers by U.S. law firms for their foreign and domestic offices. These two changes are reshaping the U.S. legal market and, in certain locations, the foreign legal market as well. They are the subject of this chapter.

---

3. *Lawyers Go Global*, ECONOMIST, Feb. 26, 2000, at 79.
4. *See* Silver, *supra* note 2, at 1128-29.

To examine these changes, I have investigated the largest and most international U.S. law firms that operate foreign offices.[5] These firms provide a venue for the changes discussed here. The work and strategies of these firms provide motivation and justification for both the increases in foreign offices and the integration of foreign lawyers into the firms. I have chronicled the foreign office activities of 71 of the largest and most international U.S. law firms from the late nineteenth century, when the first foreign offices were opened, through January 2000, using Martindale-Hubbell Directories to track the opening, closing, and staffing of foreign offices. The 71 firms at the end of this chapter (the "listed firms") were selected because they were included in the 1999 American Lawyer 100 and Global 50 lists or the International Financial Law Review's selection of the most international law firms for 1999,[6] and they each supported at least one office outside the United States in January 2000.

B. THE FIRMS: A U.S. PERSPECTIVE

Originally, U.S. law firms established foreign offices in order to practice U.S. law overseas. Foreign offices housed U.S. lawyers, and a careful line was drawn between practicing the law of the nation where the office was located and advising on U.S. law. This separation between advising on the host country's law and practicing U.S. law was required by local rules governing the activities of non-host country lawyers in most foreign office locations. In addition, foreign offices were used by U.S. law firms to follow their clients and would-be clients into foreign markets, where they proposed to continue the service already being provided in the United States. Consequently, the best training for a lawyer who wanted to work in an overseas office was essentially the same as that for any other U.S. lawyer.

During the early period of international expansion and until the mid-1980s, foreign offices were established by U.S. firms for one of two reasons. First, foreign offices were opened to serve the foreign operations of a

---

5.   *See* Silver, *supra* note 2, for additional data on the foreign office activities of the listed law firms. Unless otherwise noted, all data contained in this article on the size of foreign offices and the education of lawyers in those offices was obtained from Martindale-Hubbell Directories, using entries for the law firms' home cities, and from Martindale-Hubbell online, <http://www.marhub.com>.

6.   *The Am Law 100: By The Numbers*, AM. LAW., July 1999, at 95-135; *The Global 50*, AM. LAW., Nov. 1998, at 44-48; Euromoney Legal Training, *International Financial Law Review's 1000 Survey 1999* (visited May 13, 2000) <http://www.lawmoney.com/public/contents/latesttables/IFLR/league/1.html>.

firm's clients. Firms opened foreign offices in the same cities where their existing clients conducted or planned to conduct business. The second reason for establishing foreign offices was more personal and related to a firm's partners. Certain firms attracted lawyers with significant foreign connections or interests, or both. Most firms that claimed an international orientation early in their development followed this second pattern in establishing their first foreign offices; Coudert Brothers is one example, in which the founding partners had preexisting family and business connections in France. In other firms, partners developed strong international ties or were brought into a firm because of those ties. These two reasons for establishing foreign offices are not mutually exclusive; different foreign offices of a single law firm might well have been established for different reasons, so that both patterns may be visible within a particular firm. As a consequence, the foreign offices of most of the 71 listed law firms appear to have been established less because of a law firm's strategic business plan than as a result of generally opportunistic behavior.

During the 1980s, when client loyalties were being tested, foreign offices served as a method of maintaining control over a client's worldwide business. Firms sought protection from the risk of losing a client's work because of location, and consequently more firms opened more foreign offices. At the same time, U.S. law firms began to open foreign offices for the additional reason that they felt the need to present the image of an international law firm. As more firms seek to market themselves as international, there has been a shift in the approach to foreign offices, from opportunistic and demand-driven overseas expansion to strategies that include using overseas expansion as a mechanism for maintaining a firm's status both among its U.S. competitors and in relation to the pool of potential clients.

This shift from the client-driven and opportunistic foreign expansion of law firms that characterized the early period through the mid-1980s to the use of foreign offices as a strategy for building an international identity is evident in the growth of the number of firms with foreign offices and in the increasing number of foreign offices. Nineteen of the 71 firms listed at the end of this chapter did not enter the foreign office market until 1985 or later. Eighteen of these new entrants were firms based in U.S. cities outside of New York. Skadden Arps was the only New York firm of the listed firms that entered the foreign office market in the post-1985 period. In addition to the participation of new firms in the foreign office market, the number of foreign offices opened between 1985 and 2000 increased. The 1986 Martindale-Hubbell listings for the 71 listed firms (which reports on firms' 1985 activities) reveal that 43 firms supported 117 foreign offices. Foreign offices belonging to nine additional firms had previously been opened and closed by 1986; these firms again had at least one open foreign office in January 2000. By the beginning of 2000, a total of 343 foreign offices were supported by the 71 firms. This growth in the total number of foreign offices corresponds to an increase in the number of foreign offices supported by individual firms. In 1985, 58 percent of those firms with foreign offices had only one foreign office; by January 2000, only 18 percent of the firms supported just a single foreign branch. Clearly, the foreign office market is booming.

C. THE SIZE OF FOREIGN OFFICES

Until recently, it was common for foreign offices of U.S. law firms to be thinly staffed outposts where a firm's established clients could find a welcoming American voice. In addition to providing a "meet and greet" function, these foreign offices generated new business for the home office, the traditional "inbound" international work of advising foreign enterprises on their U.S. activities. Foreign-posted lawyers also engaged in general corporate work with an international twist: their clients were multinational companies with operations in the foreign country. The locally based employees of the multinational brought their immigration, estate planning, and other legal issues to the foreign office U.S. lawyer. The corporate entity sought legal advice on structuring relationships with local businesses in accordance with local legal regulations and business practices, which involved issues related to franchise, licensing, joint ventures, partnerships, corporations, and other areas of law. Disputes involving the client were referred to the foreign office for advice in selecting local counsel, when necessary. The client's financial needs for support of its foreign operations required the foreign office lawyer to advise on transactions involving banking law, securities regulation, and perhaps bankruptcy as well. The variety of work generated by a multinational corporation's foreign operations is as great as the variety of businesses operated by multinational companies, and the lawyer serving them must be both a generalist and a specialist. The very small number of lawyers in a foreign office required each lawyer to have sufficient expertise in his or her specialty to assume total responsibility for work in that area without support or supervision. At the same time, the variety of work brought to the foreign office lawyer, from estate planning to joint ventures, required a generalist whose broad experience and big-picture understanding enabled him or her to tackle any project that was not clearly within the expertise of another lawyer in the office. This traditional work of a foreign office generally could be and often was accomplished by a small legal staff. The small size of the foreign office was both a consequence and a cause of the nature of the work performed by its lawyers. Meager staffing policies dictated that foreign offices generally could not engage in a complex and cutting-edge international financial practice.

Evidence of the thin staffing policy is visible in the 1986 Martindale-Hubbell listings for London offices of the listed law firms. There were 29 London offices reported open in 1986. At least 20 of these offices (nearly 70 percent) were staffed with five or fewer lawyers.[7] Five offices supported between six and ten lawyers; only one office had more than ten lawyers—Baker & McKenzie's London office.

This slim staffing practice now has been discontinued in many foreign office locations. The crucial role played by the capital markets in today's economy has brought an increased role for law and lawyers generally, and U.S. lawyers have benefited especially because of the role of U.S. securities markets and financial services actors in the global economy. Lawyers in foreign offices today engage in sophisticated financial practices at the same time that they continue to serve the multinationals and their employees. The addition of a sophisticated financial practice requires and supports larger legal staffs as well as more specialized legal expertise. Moreover, in order to be both profitable and competitive, foreign offices must support a sufficient number of lawyers to enable the office to work on several transactions at one time. As a result, foreign offices in many locations are trying to hire more lawyers.

The size of foreign offices also has been influenced by a loosening of national regulations of domestic and foreign lawyers in certain locations. Regulations controlled entry by foreign lawyers into a national market as well as the extent of permissible relations between foreign and local lawyers. It is the second of these types of regulations that is relevant here. England was the first, in 1990, to remove the ban on solicitors practicing

---

7.   There is some uncertainty about staffing in less than 10% of London offices because several firms do not publish complete biographical information about their associates.

with foreign lawyers. Germany followed suit in 1995, and there has been a recent controlled loosening in Singapore, among other countries. These changes bring foreign law firms into more direct competition with local firms, both for lawyers and for clients.

The impact of these changes on foreign office staffing is perhaps most obvious in the London offices of U.S. firms. The number of lawyers in the London offices of the listed firms that were open in both 1986 and 2000 increased from 148 to 678, an increase of over 450 percent. By 2000, more than 78 percent of the 71 listed firms in my study supported a London office. More than half of these offices supported legal staffs larger than ten lawyers, with most of these concentrated in the 11- to 30-lawyer size range. At least seven firms reported legal staffs larger than 30 lawyers. These larger offices create staffing demands that are difficult to satisfy by rotating U.S. lawyers through foreign offices; at the same time, the increase in demand for lawyers created opportunities for English solicitors, who were new participants in U.S. law firms.

D. LAWYERS IN FOREIGN OFFICES

Who are the lawyers that these foreign offices are attracting? This question raises important issues for any U.S. lawyer considering an overseas assignment, and for many foreign-educated lawyers as well. The hiring patterns of foreign offices changed significantly during the 1990s, as U.S. firms increased the size of their foreign office legal staffs. Historically, U.S. firms dispatched U.S. lawyers to their foreign offices, and in many locations local lawyers were prohibited from working with U.S. and other foreign lawyers. These restrictions were lifted in the 1990s in several locations, as already described. At the same time, U.S. firms could not satisfy the staffing needs of larger foreign offices by relying exclusively on lawyers sent over for several years from the United States, and very few U.S. lawyers wanted to settle permanently in a foreign location. Moreover, significant dilemmas, discussed below, persistently confront U.S. lawyers considering an overseas assignment. Consequently, firms added foreign-educated and -licensed lawyers to their foreign legal staffs both to satisfy increased staffing needs and to add local legal expertise. The addition of foreign-educated lawyers also is present in the New York offices of many of the listed firms.

1. U.S. Lawyers in Foreign Offices

The traditional ideal candidate for a foreign office assignment is easy to imagine. They are young partners and associates with training in a major U.S. office in mergers and acquisitions, banking, securities, capital markets, and related specialties. For associates, the accepted wisdom is that several years working in the United States with experienced partners is necessary to familiarize them with basic practices of the firm and basic issues of their specialty. After this minimal period in a sophisticated practice group, mid-level associates are capable of working with less supervision in a foreign office with fewer lawyers. They will have developed a familiarity with the businesses of the firm's major clients in their specialty, and will know sufficient individual senior associates and partners to call in help should they need it. In addition, they likely will not have developed important client responsibilities at so early a stage in their careers, avoiding a significant complication of an overseas assignment.

Lawyers often begin assessing their career options after several years in practice, and as career options for lawyers with several years' experience increase, it is more difficult for firms to retain mid-level associates. The potential rewards of business and especially "dot.com" companies have lured many lawyers away from the practice of law. For those associates who consider pursuing partnership at their law firms, the career implications of an overseas assignment are uncertain. Will they be able to return to their original office if they so choose and continue on their path toward partnership? Will they be less marketable in the United States should they decide to leave the firm? In many firms, there is insufficient experience to answer these questions. Consequently, lawyers who decide to pursue partnerships in large U.S. firms often do not consider foreign office assignments advisable options.

An overseas assignment presents additional challenges for more senior lawyers. Most firms have or plan to have at least one, and often several, U.S. partners stationed in each overseas office. For these partners, whose early years generally were spent in the United States at a major law firm, how will an overseas assignment affect their careers? Will an overseas move sever client relationships? Will the lawyer be able to return to her or his original office when the foreign tour of duty is completed? How will the firm reintegrate a partner into current clients upon his or her return? These are difficult issues, and most U.S. firms in my study have no strategies for resolving these problems, much less thoughtful plans for reintegration and practice support. Lawyers who return to the United States after several years in a foreign office often struggle with the re-entry to their original or new practice locations.

Certain foreign offices recently began recruiting new U.S. law school graduates. Firms justify this practice by pointing to a foreign office's larger legal staff, which enables transactions to be staffed by more than one lawyer, thus leading to a greater capacity to train new lawyers. The larger size of a foreign office also enhances its ability to provide a steady diet of challenging legal work. Good training requires a combination of office size, a steady and reliable flow of legal work, and senior staff; the office must have a sufficient cadre of U.S.-trained lawyers to offer that training to new graduates. This combination of elements is present in only a few offices in the major business centers overseas, notably in London and Paris. For new graduates, accepting an overseas assignment as the first practice experience may be risky. U.S. lawyers are valued in the foreign market precisely because they are *U.S.* lawyers. It is their training and approach to business problems that distinguishes them from their foreign-educated colleagues, if anything. New graduates who do not receive that training risk diluting their value.

2. The Roles of Foreign Lawyers

At the same time that the global economy shifted toward financing in the public market, and as foreign offices of U.S. firms began increasing their legal staffs, two developments combined to make foreign lawyers more valuable to U.S. law firms with international practices. First, national restrictions against different nationally licensed lawyers working together in one law firm were lifted or loosened. In England, for example, in 1990, legislation was adopted permitting solicitors to form multinational partnerships, and U.S. firms began hiring solicitors as partners and associates. The solicitors brought both deal expertise and English law expertise to the U.S. firms. The changes in England's regulation of the relationship of English and foreign lawyers set the course for similar liberalization in other countries.

The second development that contributed to heightened value of foreign lawyers to U.S. law firms was the increased popularity of U.S. law schools' LL.M. programs for foreign lawyers. The 1990s brought a continually burgeoning number of foreign lawyers to the United States for education and training opportunities. U.S. law schools created and expanded existing postgraduate degree programs for these lawyers. Indeed, the number of LL.M. degree programs increased so substantially during the 1990s that the ABA

Section on Legal Education and Admission to the Bar issued a warning letter to state bar examiners explaining that the section does not separately accredit or evaluate the LL.M. programs of accredited law schools.[8]

When foreign lawyers begin their U.S. legal studies, they typically explain that they are pursuing the U.S. LL.M. degree in order to expand their opportunities in their home countries. They expect that U.S. legal education will help them in their existing legal practices or enable them to find work new opportunities. Some articulate a desire to work for a foreign law firm in their home country. Others temporarily have left jobs in which they work regularly with U.S. lawyers, such as in-house counsel for multinational corporations. They are unanimous in their view that law and lawyers, specifically lawyers trained in the United States, are playing a central role in the new economy that is reshaping their nations.

After earning the LL.M. degree, many foreign lawyers decide that they want to work in the United States for a limited period of time before returning to their home countries. They look to this possibility as a way to use their new learning, as well as an opportunity to collect the high salaries paid by U.S. law firms. It is difficult for many of these foreign lawyers with LL.M. degrees to successfully navigate the U.S. legal market. The LL.M. degree is insufficient to allow graduates to sit for the bar exam in many states, which restricts job opportunities in these states to J.D. graduates. New York is the most important exception to this general rule. In July 1998, for example, 1,371 foreign lawyers sat for the bar exam in New York; 860 of these lawyers had completed an LL.M. program in the United States.

A number of internationally oriented U.S. law firms have established foreign associate training programs to accommodate LL.M. graduates and other foreign lawyers. Some of these programs began as a result of loose affiliations between U.S. and foreign law firms. The duration of the training programs varies from several months to one year, and they are vastly oversubscribed. Training programs occasionally lead to permanent positions in law firms. Apart from the opportunities for foreign lawyers in training programs, there is a small but increasing movement among New York firms and the New York offices of non–New York U.S. firms to hire foreign-educated lawyers as regular associates.[9]

---

8.   The letter is reproduced at <http://www.abanet.org/legaled/postjdprograms/postjd_letter.html> (visited Sept. 14, 2000).

9.   The vast majority of opportunities for foreign lawyers to work in the U.S. appear to be located in New York. Only four of the 48 U.S. positions listed in the New York Univer-

Nearly all law schools separate the recruiting activities for LL.M. students from the on-campus interview programs for J.D. students. Many foreign lawyer LL.M. students approach the U.S. job market through participation in one of two annual recruiting conferences for foreign lawyers and individual letter-writing campaigns. The recruiting conferences, however, are monopolized by efforts to hire LL.M. graduates to work overseas. The January 2001 International Student Interview Program hosted by New York University School of Law, for example, included 103 potential employers advertising for 547 positions. But only 48 of the 547 jobs were located in the United States, and five of these were temporary internships. Twenty-two of the 71 listed law firms participated in this conference; 14 of these advertised openings for foreign lawyers in their U.S. offices.[10]

In spite of the intense competition for U.S. jobs, increasing numbers of foreign lawyers are working in the United States, particularly in New York. At least 42 of the 71 listed firms count foreign lawyer LL.M. graduates among the ranks of their lawyers in their New York offices, either as participants in a foreign lawyer training program or as regular associates or partners.[11] Certain firms, including Morrison & Foerster, Graham & James, and Winston & Strawn, also employ foreign lawyers in domestic

---

sity 2001 International Student Interviewing Program were for positions outside of New York; an additional five positions were listed for the United States generally, with no specific location noted. See note 10, infra, for additional information on the New York University program.

10.   Compare the preliminary information for the January 2000 International Student Interview Program at NYU, which included 106 potential employers advertising for 459 positions. Only 49 of the 459 jobs were located in the United States, and two of those were temporary internships. Twenty-five of the 71 listed law firms participated in the 2000 NYU conference; 19 of these advertised openings for foreign lawyers in their U.S. offices. The following listed firms participated in the NYU conference in the year indicated; an asterisk indicates that the firm advertised for jobs in the United States: Akin Gump ('00, '01), Altheimer & Gray ('00, '01), Baker & McKenzie ('00*, '01), Brown & Wood ('00*), Cleary Gottlieb ('00,* '01), Coudert Brothers ('00,* '01*), Davis Polk ('00,* '01*), Debevoise & Plimpton ('00*, '01*), Dewey Ballantine ('00*), Dorsey & Whitney ('00*), Gibson Dunn ('00,* '01*), Hogan & Hartson ('00), Hunton & Williams ('00), Jones Day ('00,* '01), Latham & Watkins (01*), Mayer Brown & Platt ('00,* '01*), Milbank Tweed ('00,* '01*), Morgan Lewis ('00,* '01), Morrison & Foerster ('00,*), Paul Weiss Rifkind Wharton & Garrison ('01*), Shearman & Sterling ('00,* '01*), Sidley & Austin ('00,* '01*), Simpson, Thacher & Bartlett ('01*), Skadden ('00, '01), Sullivan & Cromwell ('00,* '01*), White & Case ('00,* '01*), Willkie Farr ('00, '01), and Wilmer Cutler & Pickering ('00,* '01).

11.   This number may be artificially low because of the absence of biographical information about associates in several law firms.

offices outside of New York. For most firms, the introduction of foreign lawyer LL.M. graduates has been accomplished on an ad hoc basis and is clearly an exception to the general requirement that lawyers earn a J.D. degree from a U.S. law school. The hiring partner at one of the listed firms recently confided that his firm has absolutely no policy on hiring foreign lawyers with or without a U.S. LL.M. degree, and during the same conversation discovered that his firm employed at least six foreign lawyers in the United States.

The LL.M. degree is crucial for civil law lawyers attempting to secure a position in the United States. The degree enables civil law–trained lawyers to take the New York bar examination, and consequently functions almost as a prerequisite for employment in the United States. An example is revealing: Davis Polk & Wardwell's Web site lists among its lawyers in its New York office 25 lawyers who had not earned a J.D degree in the United States.[12] Sixteen of these are common law–trained lawyers, ten of whom also have earned an LL.M. or M.C.L. degree at a U.S. law school. In comparison, each of the nine civil law–trained lawyers working at Davis Polk has earned an LL.M. in the United States.

For foreign lawyers trained in a common law jurisdiction, the LL.M. is less important. New York's bar rules permit these lawyers to take the bar examination without additional U.S. legal education, and lawyers from Canada, the U.K., Australia, and New Zealand are becoming an accepted minority in large-firm New York offices. In fact, several Wall Street firms have added law schools in these jurisdictions to their annual on-campus interviewing sites.

U.S. law firms find foreign lawyers with LL.M. degrees particularly desirable for their foreign offices. They bring a thorough understanding of their home country legal systems, an appreciation of U.S. law, and perhaps helpful contacts in the host country as well. And they solve one of the persistent difficulties of staffing foreign offices because they will remain in the foreign location indefinitely, thus alleviating the need to periodically rotate additional lawyers through the foreign office.

Foreign-licensed lawyers play a more significant role in the foreign offices of U.S. law firms now than they did 25 years ago. In 1986, English solicitors were not permitted to work as partners or employees of foreign lawyers. Nevertheless, two of the listed law firms included English solici-

---

12.   See Davis Polk & Wardwell Web site, <http://www.dpw/lawyers/alpha.com> (July 5, 2000).

tors as counsel and one firm included an English solicitor as an associate lawyer in their London offices. Three additional listed firms employed lawyers admitted in the U.S. and also as English solicitors. In each of these six offices, the English solicitors worked alongside U.S.-licensed lawyers. More than 60 percent of the London offices of the listed firms were staffed solely by U.S.-licensed lawyers in 1986. Only one office, that of Baker & McKenzie, employed a greater number of foreign-licensed lawyers than U.S.-licensed lawyers in 1986.

By 2000, the number of London offices of the listed firms where the entire legal staff is composed of lawyers admitted only in the United States had decreased from more than 60 percent to 21 percent. Twenty-one of the 56 London offices open in 2000, or nearly 38 percent, employ more lawyers admitted to practice in England than U.S.-licensed lawyers, and one firm's London office employs only lawyers admitted in England. Twenty-three of the 56 firms employ lawyers who are licensed both in England and the United States. An additional 11 firms employ lawyers who were educated in the United States or England and licensed in the other country.

These changes reflect the liberalization of regulations of solicitors and foreign lawyers, as well as the added breadth of advisory expertise in these London offices. In 1986, U.S. firms were advising on U.S. law from their London offices; today, they offer expertise in both U.S. and English law. Similarly, lawyers with U.S. and English law expertise staff English law firms with New York offices. As a result, the competition between the U.S. and English firms has increased considerably. They compete for business, for lawyers, and for their law to be adopted as governing particular transactions.

Germany provides a more extreme picture of the role of foreign lawyers in U.S. firms' foreign offices. Fourteen of the listed firms supported 20 offices in Germany, 19 of which were established between 1989 and 1999. Only two of these offices (10 percent), both located in Frankfurt, are staffed solely by lawyers who were educated and admitted to practice only in the United States; this is half the proportion of English offices that were staffed solely by U.S. lawyers. All of the lawyers in eight offices are German Rechtsanwalt; in six of these offices many of the Rechtsanwalt also are admitted in the United States or England. In seven additional offices, German Rechtsanwalt outnumber the lawyers who are licensed in only the United States, Canada, or England. Thus, 65 percent of the offices are dominated by German-educated and -licensed lawyers, compared to 38 percent of the English offices, as noted above. Seventy-five percent of the listed firms' offices in Germany host lawyers who are either dual educated or licensed, or both, in the United States and Germany.

This information reveals the importance of German law expertise in the work of the German offices of U.S. law firms. German offices are more dominated by German lawyers than are English offices dominated by English lawyers. The differences between staffing in London and Germany may decrease as the German offices mature, and the mergers of German and English law firms also may impact staffing in U.S. firms' German offices. Current office staffing in Germany clearly reveals that the U.S. firms are doing more than advising on U.S. law.

E. CONCLUSION

Historically, lawyers working in the foreign offices of U.S. law firms practiced U.S. law. That fact dictated that the best preparation for a foreign office assignment was a basic U.S. legal education along with several years of experience at a large U.S. law firm. Many U.S. law firms today offer expertise in U.S. and foreign law, and foreign offices reflect this change. In addition, foreign offices are involved in more sophisticated and substantive practices.

These changes have required U.S. firms to revise their foreign office staffing practices. U.S. lawyers continue to be valued and critical members of the foreign office team, and the demand for them should motivate firms to address the uncertainties attached to an overseas assignment. But in addition to U.S. lawyers, foreign-trained lawyers populate foreign offices. Some of these foreign lawyers have earned U.S. LL.M. degrees; English legal education, too, is quite common among lawyers in civil law and other common law countries. Foreign offices also house a small number of lawyers who were educated and licensed in a third country apart from the United States and the foreign office location.

Of course, the most common foreign lawyers in U.S. law firms in any particular location are those at home in that location, and their familiarity with the host country benefits the firm and its clients. The success of commercial and legal activities is intimately tied to local history and the local economic and political system. Ben Heineman of General Electric eloquently articulated this point:

So much of practicing law these days outside of the United States is understanding the economic and political system, not just the legal system. I think we should not confine ourselves to a narrow view of the law. You simply can't practice law in a country unless you have people there who understand the history and the culture. If we look around the world, legal arrangements are fine, but most of the countries don't have legal systems that are very durable, that provide much certainty. That is probably one of the greatest challenges we face: How do we structure arrangements in countries where the legal system is, to a great extent, undeveloped? It is for that reason that you have to have people who are skilled in the culture and the history of the society.[13]

Globalization may encourage the harmonization of national legal systems, but it does not erase all local differences that have the potential to impact business and commercial interests; it simply makes the differences subtler. Foreign-trained lawyers' understanding of these subtleties adds a valuable element to the advisory capacities of U.S. law firms.

THE LISTED FIRMS

(Home office location is indicated in parentheses.)
1. Akin, Gump, Strauss, Hauer & Feld (Dallas)
    1700 Pacific Ave., Suite 4100, Dallas, TX 75201
    www.akingump.com
2. Altheimer & Gray (Chicago)
    10 S. Wacker Dr., Suite 4000, Chicago, IL 60606
    www.altheimer.com
3. Arnold & Porter (Washington, D.C.)
    555 12th St. NW, Washington, DC 20004
    www.aporter.com
4. Baker Botts (Houston)
    One Shell Plaza, 910 Louisiana St., Houston, TX 77002
    www.bakerbotts.com
5. Baker & McKenzie (Chicago)
    One Prudential Plaza, 130 E. Randolph Drive, Chicago, IL 60601
    www.bakernet.com

---

13.   *Global Roundtable: Taking on the World*, Am. Law., Nov. 1998, at 97, 105-06.

6. Bingham Dana (Boston)
    150 Federal St., Boston, MA 02110
    www.bingham.com

7. Brobeck, Phleger & Harrison (San Francisco)
    One Market, Spear Street Tower, San Francisco, CA 94105
    www.brobeck.com

8. Brown & Wood (New York)
    One World Trade Center, New York, NY 10048
    www.brownwoodlaw.com

9. Bryan Cave (St. Louis)
    211 North Broadway, St. Louis, MO 63102
    www.Bryancavellp.com

10. Cadwalader, Wickersham & Taft (New York)
    100 Maiden Ln., New York, NY 10038, cadwalader.com

11. Cahill, Gordon & Reindel (New York)
    80 Pine St., New York, NY 10005
    www.cahill.com

12. Chadbourne & Parke (New York)
    30 Rockefeller Plaza, New York, NY 10112
    www.chadbourne.com

13. Cleary, Gottlieb, Steen & Hamilton (New York)
    One Liberty Plaza, New York, NY 10006
    www.cgsh.com

14. Coudert Brothers (New York)
    1114 Avenue of the Americas, New York, NY 10036
    www.coudert.com

15. Covington & Burling (Washington, D.C.)
    1200 Pennsylvania Ave. NW, Washington, DC 20004
    www.cov.com

16. Cravath, Swaine & Moore (New York)
    Worldwide Plaza, 825 Eighth Ave., New York, NY 10019
    www.cravath.com

17. Curtis Mallet-Prevost Colt & Mosle (New York)
    101 Park Ave., New York, NY 10178
    www.cm-p.com

18. Davis Polk & Wardwell (New York)
    450 Lexington Ave., New York, NY 10017
    www.dpw.com

19. Debevoise & Plimpton (New York)
     875 Third Ave., 25th Floor, New York, NY 10022
     www.debevoise.com
20. Dechert Price & Rhoads (Philadelphia)
     (recently merged with Titmuss Sainer Dechert)
     4000 Bell Atlantic Tower, 1717 Arch St.,
     Philadelphia, PA 19103-2793
     www.dechert.com
21. Dewey Ballantine (New York)
     1301 Avenue of the Americas, New York, NY 10019
     www.deweyballantine.com
22. Dorsey & Whitney (Minneapolis)
     220 S. 6th St., Minneapolis, MN 55402
     www.dorseylaw.com
23. Faegre & Benson (Minneapolis)
     90 S. Seventh St., Minneapolis, MN 55402
     www.faegre.com
24. Foley & Lardner (Milwaukee)
     Firstar Center, 777 E. Wisconsin Ave., Milwaukee, WI 53202
     www.foleylardner.com
25. Fried, Frank, Harris, Shriver & Jacobson (New York)
     One New York Plaza, New York, NY 10004
     www.ffhsj.com
26. Fulbright & Jaworski (Houston)
     1301 McKinney St., Suite 5100, Houston, TX 77010
     www.fulbright.com
27. Gibson, Dunn & Crutcher (Los Angeles)
     333 S. Grand Ave., Los Angeles, CA 90071
     gibsondunn.com
28. Graham & James (San Francisco)[14]
     (now merged with Squire, Sanders & Dempsey LLP)
     One Maritime Plaza, Suite 300, San Francisco, CA 94111
     www.ssd.com

---

14.   The association of Graham & James with Deacons in Hong Kong and Australia ended on July 1, 2000; the firm's Hong Kong and Australian offices became part of Deacons. Letter from Paul Scholefield & Lindsay B. Esler, partners at Deacons Graham & James, Hong Kong (Apr. 5, 2000) (on file with author).

29. Heller Ehrman White & McAuliffe (San Francisco)
    333 Bush St., San Francisco, CA 94104
    www.hewm.com
30. Hogan & Hartson (Washington, D.C.)
    Columbia Square, 555 13th St. NW, Washington, DC 20004
    www.hhlaw.com
31. Hughes Hubbard & Reed (New York)
    One Battery Park Plaza, New York, NY 10004
    www.hugheshubbard.com
32. Hunton & Williams (Richmond)
    Riverfront Plaza, East Tower, 951 E. Byrd St., Richmond, VA 23219
    www.hunton.com
33. Jones, Day, Reavis & Pogue (Cleveland)
    901 Lakeside Ave., Cleveland, OH 44114
    www.jonesday.com
34. Kaye, Scholer, Fierman, Hays & Handler (New York)
    425 Park Ave., New York, NY 10022
    www.kayescholer.com
35. Kelley Drye & Warren (New York)
    101 Park Ave., New York, NY 10178
    www.kelleydrye.com
36. Kilpatrick Stockton (Atlanta)
    1100 Peachtree St. NE, Suite 2800, Atlanta, GA 30309
    www.kilstock.com
37. Kirkland & Ellis (Chicago)
    Aon Center, 200 E. Randolph Dr., Chicago, IL 60601
    www.kirkland.com
38. Latham & Watkins (Los Angeles)
    633 W. Fifth St., Suite 4000, Los Angeles, CA 90071
    www.lw.com
39. LeBoeuf, Lamb, Greene & MacRae (New York)
    125 W. 55th St., New York, NY 10019
    www.llgm.com
40. Mayer, Brown & Platt (Chicago)
    190 S. LaSalle St., Chicago, IL 60603
    www.mayerbrown.com

41. McCutchen, Doyle, Brown & Enersen (San Francisco)
     Three Embarcadero Center, San Francisco, CA 94111
     www.mccutchen.com

42. McDermott, Will & Emery (Chicago)
     227 W. Monroe St., Chicago, IL 60606
     www.mwe.com

43. McGuire Woods Battle & Boothe (Richmond)
     One James Center, 901 E. Cary St., Richmond, VA 23219
     www.mwbb.com

44. Milbank, Tweed, Hadley & McCloy (New York)
     One Chase Manhattan Plaza, New York, NY 10005
     www.milbank.com

45. Morgan, Lewis & Bockius (Philadelphia)
     1701 Market St., Philadelphia, PA 19103-2921
     www.morganlewis.com

46. Morrison & Foerster (San Francisco)
     425 Market St., San Francisco CA 94105
     www.mofo.com

47. O'Melveny & Myers (Los Angeles)
     400 S. Hope St., Los Angeles, CA 90071
     www.omm.com

48. Orrick, Herrington & Sutcliffe (San Francisco)
     Old Federal Reserve Bank Bldg., 400 Sansome St.,
     San Francisco, CA 94111
     www.orrick.com

49. Paul, Hastings, Janofsky & Walker (Los Angeles)
     555 S. Flower St., Los Angeles, CA 90071
     www.phjw.com

50. Paul, Weiss, Rifkind, Wharton & Garrison (New York)
     1285 Avenue of the Americas, New York, NY 10019
     www.paulweiss.com

51. Perkins Coie (Seattle)
     1201 Third Ave., Fl 40, Seattle, WA 98101
     www.perkinscoie.com

52. Pillsbury Madison & Sutro (San Francisco)
     50 Fremont St., San Francisco, CA 94105
     pillsburywinthrop.com

53. Proskauer Rose (New York)
     1585 Broadway, New York, NY 10036
     www.proskauer.com
54. Seyfarth, Shaw, Fairweather & Geraldson (Chicago)
     55 E. Monroe St., Suite 4200, Chicago, IL 60603
     www.seyfarth.com
55. Shaw Pittman (Washington, D.C.)
     2300 N Street NW, Washington, DC 20037
     www.shawpittman.com
56. Shearman & Sterling (New York)
     599 Lexington Ave., New York, NY 10022
     www.shearman.com
57. Shook, Hardy & Bacon (Kansas City)
     One Kansas City Pl., 1200 Main St., Kansas City, MO 64105
     www.shb.com
58. Sidley & Austin (Chicago)
     Bank One Plaza, 10 S. Dearborn St., Chicago, IL 60603
     www.sidley.com
59. Simpson Thacher & Bartlett (New York)
     425 Lexington Ave., New York, NY 10017
     www.stblaw.com
60. Skadden, Arps, Slate, Meagher & Flom (New York)
     Four Times Square, New York, NY 10036
     www.sasmf.com
61. Squire, Sanders & Dempsey (Cleveland)
     4900 Key Tower, 127 Public Square, Cleveland, OH 44114
     www.ssd.com
62. Stroock & Stroock & Lavan (New York)
     180 Maiden Ln., New York, NY 10038
     www.stroock.com
63. Sullivan & Cromwell (New York)
     125 Broad St., New York, NY 10004
     www.sullcrom.com
64. Vinson & Elkins (Houston)
     2300 First City Tower, 1001 Fannin, Houston, TX 77002
     www.vinson-elkins.com

65. Weil, Gotshal & Manges (New York)
    767 Fifth Ave., New York, NY 10153
    www.weil.com

66. White & Case (New York)
    1155 Avenue of the Americas, New York, NY 10036
    www.whitecase.com

67. Willkie Farr & Gallagher (New York)
    787 Seventh Ave., New York, NY 10019
    www.willkie.com

68. Wilmer, Cutler & Pickering (Washington, D.C.)
    2445 M St. NW, Washington, DC 20037
    www.wilmer.com

69. Wilson, Elser, Moskowitz, Edelman & Dicker (New York)
    150 E. 42nd St., New York, NY 10017
    www.wemed.com

70. Winston & Strawn (Chicago)
    35 W. Wacker Dr., Chicago, IL 60601
    www.winston.com

71. Winthrop, Stimson, Putnam & Roberts (New York)
    (now merged with Pillsbury Madison & Sutro)
    One Battery Park Plaza, New York, NY 10004
    www.winstim.com

Using the Internet to Run a Small-Firm International Business Law Practice

2

by Jeffrey M. Aresty and Andrew S. Breines

A. INTRODUCTION

How would you like to set up your own international law office? Do you want to travel around the world and work with people from many different cultures while navigating the shoals of many legal systems? Most law students aren't thinking of a career path that can lead to almost anyplace on the planet. It's not only possible; in the years ahead, this path will expand for many law students who choose to pursue an international law career and are prepared to work among the cultures of the world.

Most law schools are just now adding courses to beef up their international law offerings. E-commerce law, the newest, is the most important in a practice like ours. However, this doesn't entirely prepare you for a career representing entrepreneurial clients in a global setting. As emerging technologies become more important in defining new ways of practicing law over the Internet, bright young law students will have more chances than ever before to pursue careers in small-firm settings practicing private international law.

Most law students conceive of a career in international law as working in a large law firm in a cosmopolitan city, working for the U.S. government in a trade or diplomatic role, or working as legal counsel to a large multinational corporation. In recent years many types of small international business law firms have opened up and provide a new career opportunity. There are international law "boutiques," which cater to legal specialties such as customs or trade law. There also are general international business law firms, like our firm.

Our practice consists of two partners, two of counsel, and a worldwide network of professional service providers and contacts, which we have built up over the years by becoming active in international associations and chambers of commerce. We represent U.S. business interests overseas and foreign interests in the United States. We have to be familiar with the business laws and customs of many cultures. Because we are small, we use our Rolodex® to assemble "built to order" teams to handle the needs of our international clientele.

B. WORKING IN A GLOBAL ENVIRONMENT

After 23 years of working at the crossroads of many of the world's cultures, we constantly must learn new ways to work successfully in a global environment. In the future, this ability will be even more important as the Internet rapidly brings everyone in the world together through e-commerce. This is a particularly significant development for law students who can be at the forefront of using new technologies, then can enter law firms searching for new lawyers who have this skill set to join their team.

These are some of the ways that the Internet is changing the practice of law. Virtual collaboration over the Web is the key tool. Why? Having instant access to your legal team and being able to remain in contact from virtually anywhere in the world is a great timesaver as law firms reduce the complexity involved when many firms are working on the same matter. We embrace the changes the Internet has brought. Law firms can use tools such as virtual collaboration to expand their Web presence beyond simple online brochures to an interactive presence that has the power to change their practices. The most innovative firms offer free legal information online, the ability to schedule a telephone consultation online, and a secure extranet/Web space in which their clients may communicate and collaborate at any time. This allows clients in Asia to work when they are available instead of trying to find that small window each day during which people from around the world are awake at the same time. In short, the Internet allows lawyers to offer "local delivery" of legal information to clients where and when the client needs the information. Students who embrace this technology while they are in law school will have a distinct advantage over those who think that the Internet is just a research tool.

C. TWO EXAMPLES OF HOW OUR FIRM USED THE INTERNET EFFECTIVELY WITH FOREIGN CLIENTS

The following are two case studies that explain how we used technology to deliver legal services and how the Internet's global reach affects the way our firm provides international business law services to clients located outside the United States. One client located us on the Internet through an international listing of business professionals. A colleague introduced the other client.

For the first client, we outlined the scope of services required via e-mail and telephone communications before entering into a fee agreement. Because the client is based in Canada and we are located in Boston, the Internet provided the best communications tool for this relationship. Since this Canadian client's service will be offered over the Internet to users around the world, there were several international legal issues in addition to U.S. laws that had to be reviewed. International treaties (intellectual property and arbitration) were examined. U.S and Canadian securities laws were examined and reviewed in addition to specific communication with regulators in both countries. Since the client's business was somewhat novel, we were required to interpret existing law, policy, and culture in order to provide an opinion on how the regulators from different parts of the world would react. In the absence of a global rule, we had to help our client develop a globally compliant operational plan. Our virtual collaboration with the client helped us understand its service better and faster while we did the research.

A second client from the United Kingdom, referred to us via an e-mail from a colleague, had been selling its products in North America without a formal agreement for several years. We had an initial brief phone conversation at the outset of the relationship. From that point forward, the only communication was via e-mail and fax. The client explained its initial needs, which were to draft a distribution and consignment relationship, and we provided a solution. The client wanted its existing relationships with its authorized agents in North America to remain unchanged. Since these relationships were not typical, the final agreements had to be specific to this relationship, and rules in both the United States and Canada had to be addressed. Since the laws and customs of Canada are not always similar to those in the United States, we retained Canadian counsel to provide an opinion regarding Canadian law. We established a virtual collaboration among ourselves, Canadian counsel, and the client.

As it turned out, Canadian law made it extremely difficult for the Canadian relationship to remain as it had been. However, based on our knowledge of our client's business processes and practices, we were able to formalize an agreement that allowed the client and its Canadian distributor to continue to operate in a manner very similar to their past practices. Working virtually with everyone involved, we crafted a solution. Our collaboration with Canadian counsel allowed us to prepare a distribution agreement that avoided security and payment issues that the client's preferred consignment relationship would have defeated.

One other aspect of these two cases is worth pointing out to new lawyers. Building a network of contacts from the beginning of your career is important in handling global work. Joining the ABA's Section of International Law and Practice and becoming active is a great way to make these contacts.

D. WHAT ARE THE REWARDS OF A CAREER PRACTICING INTERNATIONAL BUSINESS LAW IN A SMALL FIRM?

If your personality is suited to a small firm rather than a large firm, there are many rewards for making this choice. You will be closer to the action with the clients and more directly involved in helping them solve their problems from an earlier point in your career. More of these opportunities are available on a daily basis in small-firm environments than in any other practice setting. Because most busy lawyers are constantly juggling priorities and managing big caseloads to tight deadlines, there is no part of any day where solid and talented help wouldn't be appreciated. A busy small law firm will be involved in managing business deals and complex and simple litigation for multiple clients simultaneously. In an international practice, responding to work in several jurisdictions daily for several different clients is business as usual. Just having someone around who can organize and work substantively on case files and begin responding to routine matters is an asset that most firms would greatly appreciate.

Clients appreciate personal attention from lawyers, and a young lawyer who is properly prepared on a file is a second lawyer the client can hear from on a regular basis. Learning how to communicate effectively with clients comes only from experience, and on-the-job training is the best way to learn. In fact, client contact in a small-firm setting can be a key to your personal growth as a lawyer. Clients come in all types and from all cultures in an international practice. Learning how to respond to each client will only add value to your legal career as you continue to learn and effectively manage your time and resources to the benefit of your clients.

What type of personality is right for a small, private international law practice? Perhaps the most important quality is the ability to be a self-starter who can work independently with proper guidance and mentoring. Since you will be expected to handle many different matters in multiple jurisdictions during the course of each day, week, and month, your ability to properly segment each matter while prioritizing tasks is a valuable quality to cultivate and nurture. Some prioritizing will be dictated by the partners and senior associates at your firm. In some firms, experienced secretaries and paralegals who have long-standing relationships with small international law firms do the prioritizing and scheduling. Learning how to use the professional staff of your firm properly and effectively is another skill that can only be learned through experience.

E. OUR ADVICE ON CAREER PREPARATION

There are some skills that a young lawyer will want to develop to be successful in this type of practice. These skills include an understanding of the world's cultures, the world's laws and their interaction with business practices, and an entrepreneurial attitude and outlook.

First, you will want to learn about the world's cultures. Our firm hosts law clerk interns referred by Boston-area international language schools for one-month to one-year positions. These schools provide certificate and training programs to students from other nations and cultures who want to learn English. Many of these students have prior legal backgrounds or have completed law school in their home countries and are seeking practical experience with English in a professional setting. In addition to our international law clerks, we have two lawyers who are "of counsel" who have special skills in international law and international business consulting. We participate in and organize programs for international chambers of commerce on topics of international business law and meet people from other cultures who have moved to Boston. We attend programs at law schools with an international focus.

Second, a strong working knowledge of many areas of law is crucial. These include U.S. securities and banking laws, tax laws, corporate laws, and intellectual property laws, as well as familiarity with the issues associated with drafting and reviewing international agreements. More recently, it has become important to develop a foundation of knowledge in e-commerce law. It is useful to be fluent in many legal topics that can have an impact on international business. An excellent way to do that is to purchase a copy of the ABA *International Lawyer's Deskbook*, which provides a good overview of the many issues that require consideration before performing services for an international client.

Remember that you will want to get special counsel involved when necessary to provide your clients with the best advice possible. This includes being able to locate local counsel anywhere on the globe. Having a strong working knowledge of law doesn't mean that you will practice in each of these areas; it means you will have the ability to provide your clients with advice that is specific and useful to their situation. Too many firms still rely on the "cookie-cutter approach." This means that when they are retained to work with a certain type of client, they immediately go to their "forms library" and pull out the agreement they used for a past client, revise it, and praise its blessings to the client. This approach fails to account for cultural nuances that international negotiations and agreements ultimately rely on to form lasting relationships. Our procedures allow us to learn about our clients' business processes and practices and about their counterparts so we can prepare client-specific documentation that relates directly to *their* transaction, not to some prior transaction fashioned to fit their circumstances.

Third, an entrepreneurial attitude is needed so you will be able to empathize with your clients, and your clients will feel that you understand their needs and appreciate your desire to find ways to meet their business objectives. Then, as you do your outside reading, you will be thinking of how to help your clients find new markets for their products or how to help them navigate a tricky cross-cultural negotiation.

Finally, to be a successful international business lawyer, you will need interpersonal skills to help you demonstrate that you understand your clients' legal concerns and that you can resolve them, but that many of the issues involved in international transactions contain cultural and communication obstacles that a simple document cannot overcome. Only by demonstrating your understanding of how your client and its counterpart will form a lasting relationship can you fully and completely become an international business lawyer. Small firms and solo practitioners need to be able to stand out from the pack to get and retain clients. Yes, some matters will require nothing more than preparing the appropriate documents and moving on to the next client. However, if you demonstrate your communication skills and your sense and understanding of the cultural issues, your client will be more likely to contact you for help on the next issue. Once that communication occurs, you will have successfully retained a client and formed a long-lasting professional relationship.

F. CONCLUSION

Our experience of the changing nature of the legal practice and how lawyers will deliver services in the future serve to strengthen our belief that verbal and written communication and the ability to understand a client's business are the key ingredients to succeeding as an international business lawyer in the twenty-first century. Only by embracing technology and the transformation of the way that legal services are beginning to be delivered globally can you succeed in a small or midsize international business law firm. We can't emphasize enough the influence that a young lawyer can have on the current members of a firm based on his or her experience with technology. In fact, technology could be one of the best ways to be noticed by the powers that be at the firm you join.

The International Lawyer as Conductor of the Global Symphony

3

by John P. Cogan, Jr.

A. INTRODUCTION

Individual members of the orchestra tune their instruments, creating dissonant, grating sounds. Then the conductor ascends the podium and, from the same diverse group of instruments, summons forth a unified sound of immense dimensions. So, too, must the international lawyer climb the podium and direct an international transaction involving diverse national jurisdictions, a global symphony, to a successful conclusion.

B. EARLY INTERNATIONAL LAWYERS

I date the beginnings of the international law practice, in earnest, for U.S. law firms outside of New York to the period immediately following World War II. However, such firms practiced some international law long before then. Edwin Parker, a Houston lawyer, was a member of various international claims tribunals arising out of World War I from 1918 until the middle 1920s. A random search of his firm's files disclosed correspondence with lawyers and clients in Mexico well before the turn of the nineteenth century.

The oldest international law volume I could find in Houston law firm libraries was a treatise on Mexican and Spanish Civil Law published in 1851. I cannot find an acquisition date, but it is reasonable to assume that the book was put to good use in Houston well before 1900. In fact, there was certainly some international law (public international law, at least) practiced in Houston in the days of the Republic of Texas arising out of the republic's relations with foreign governments.

So the practice of international law outside of New York is not new. What is new is the role that international law plays in our commerce and the methods utilized in the practice.

C. WHO ARE INTERNATIONAL LAWYERS TODAY?

Any lawyer who has ever handled a matter involving the laws of more than one jurisdiction is an international lawyer (and I suspect that includes all of us). On the other hand, we are all a bit reluctant to call ourselves "international" lawyers. Even if our practice is primarily international, we prefer to describe it in terms of some area of substantive law. We are corporate lawyers, banking lawyers, oil and gas lawyers, trade lawyers, customs lawyers, or lawyers specializing in other areas of substantive law. We are not international lawyers.

An American lawyer practicing in Brussels once told me there was no such person as an international lawyer. He was wrong. He was one himself; but he either did not want to admit it, did not understand it, or chose not to disclose it because he assumed nobody else would understand.

D. THE ROLE OF THE INTERNATIONAL LAW PRACTICE

1. Defining the Practice

International lawyers do exist, but it is often difficult to define their role. Indeed, their role is much like the role of a symphonic conductor. They must find methods to harmonize the cacophony of diverse, often conflicting laws of multiple jurisdictions.

a. Movement Across Frontiers

My first feeble effort to describe the practice was to say, only half in jest, that it involved any correspondence coming into our mailroom with a foreign postage stamp on it. That explanation did not really satisfy me or anybody who heard it. So I continued to seek a brief but comprehensive definition. I finally came up with one that seems so simple that I am sure you have already thought of it. To me, an international law practice is a practice that relates to the movement of people, money, goods, and ideas across international frontiers. That says it all. In fact, you might believe it says too much. But nobody expects you to know the French Code of Civil Procedure like you may once have known the words to a Beatles song. Nobody expects you to know the Bolivian Foreign Investment Code like you may know Article 9 of the Uniform Commercial Code. But, if you are a good international lawyer, you will know what questions to ask and where to find the answers. Nobody expects the symphonic conductor to know how to play all the instruments in an orchestra, but he or she will know how to read the score.

b. A Procedural Specialty

In other words, international law is primarily a procedural specialty, not a substantive one. Like the trial lawyer who offers a procedural specialty (maneuvering around courtrooms and asking the right questions of witnesses), the international lawyer offers a procedural specialty: getting around in foreign conference rooms, asking the right questions of foreign lawyers, and, most important, communicating with clients and adversaries in a manner that transcends cultural and linguistic barriers.

c. Substantive Specialty

Of course, within the framework of an international practice, there also are many substantive specialties, such as international corporate or finance law. Some lawyers may specialize substantively in the laws related to a particular foreign jurisdiction or to a particular type of activity like international trade or immigration, but they all possess that one unifying factor: they all involve movements across international frontiers.

d. International Lawyers as Generalists

A client may come to an international lawyer initially only for advice of very limited scope—for example, advice on moving goods into or out of a particular country (which is usually the bailiwick of international trade specialists). On the surface, this type of representation appears to require work with only one very specialized set of laws in one jurisdiction. However, the result in the applicable jurisdiction may well depend on how the transaction is structured in other jurisdictions to which the transaction relates. Consequently, to represent the client well, the trade specialist must have a transnational overview of the client's affairs and an overview of the jurisdictions with which the client may be involved. This requires the specialist also to become something of a generalist—a true Renaissance man.

2. Identifying the Skills

Once we know what an international practice is, we must consider what skills are necessary for that practice.

a. Enlightened Communication

In countries where literacy is limited, public scribes often can be found to serve as professional communicators for those who lack the technical skills for successful written communication. In a world of transnational commercial activities, the international lawyer plays a similar role because of his or her ability to reduce complicated issues facing the client into simple, nontechnical terms that can survive translation into the consciousness of another party from a different culture. Try explaining consequential damages to a Brazilian lawyer.

The lawyer who can communicate only in the legal jargon and boilerplate of his or her own jurisdiction, who flourishes in the use of synonyms when one term will do, who refuses to renounce laundry lists of "including but not limited to's" is a lawyer who should apply his or her drafting skills only to the conveyancing of real estate back home or to the creation of indentures for the sale of bonds to New York insurance companies.

The international lawyer realizes that it is worth the time and effort to distill a 10,000-word document into 1,000 words if the substance can be preserved in a clear fashion. Realizing that brevity and simplicity in drafting take more time, effort, and self-confidence, the international lawyer accepts the challenge. He or she realizes that to do otherwise in the international arena will result in a document that is unintelligible to at least one party and therefore damaging to all parties. Imagine a musical score that can be read by the violinists but not the flutists.

b. Languages

Is it necessary for an international lawyer to speak more than one language? Language is a powerful insight into the cultures with which the lawyer will be involved. But total fluency is not as crucial as simply a proper respect for foreign languages and for the inherent dangers of an uncritical reliance on translations.

A lawyer who is not afraid of foreign languages can overcome a lack of total fluency through the judicious use of dictionaries, grammars, comparisons of different translations, comparisons of translations with originals, and discussions with lawyers who were born and trained in the language of the original. After you become involved with the challenges of translation, you will understand the importance of my earlier point that the original must be clearly and simply drafted.

So an ability with foreign languages is important but not nearly as important as the ability to think and communicate clearly in one language. And frequently these skills are mutually exclusive. To the extent they are mutually exclusive, I would take the clear thinker over the linguist as my lawyer any day. Did you ever wonder why bellhops and taxi drivers often are great linguists while presidents and corporate executives are not?

c. Curiosity

Finally, the international law practice requires intellectual curiosity; an insatiable appetite for observing the culture, politics, and economics of other peoples; and a distaste for the security of repetitive work. The person who enjoys preparing S-8s or ERISA pension plans and prefers a weekend in Galveston to a few days in Morelia will not find happiness in devising and implementing a joint venture among German, Japanese, and American groups for the development of a copper mine in Ecuador.

E. THE METHODS OF AN INTERNATIONAL PRACTICE

1. Local Counsel in Another State

It is difficult for a lawyer to become proficient in the law and practice of more than one jurisdiction. So, in handling domestic multistate transactions, a lawyer (primary counsel) must frequently call upon a colleague (local counsel) in another state for assistance. Such assistance might include (1) help defining the questions involved, (2) finding local legal authorities to answer the questions, (3) reconciling conflicts of law, and (4) help formulating as well as implementing a plan of action based on the previous analytical work.

In any event, the two domestic lawyers' educational and cultural backgrounds as well as their methodology are likely to be similar enough that primary counsel will need to do little more than lay out the facts to local counsel in order to get the necessary help. Local counsel will even assist without much prodding (or often without a request at all) in formulating and refining the questions presented. After that, local counsel can do the job with a minimum of supervision from primary counsel.

2. Local Counsel in a Foreign Country

If multistate transactions are difficult to handle without assistance from local counsel, international transactions are virtually impossible to handle alone. Clearly, local counsel must be consulted in all but the most minor or special cases. Furthermore, the need for foreign counsel is not limited to business planning and litigation in a foreign court. It stretches to international litigation in U.S. courts where service on foreign parties and foreign discovery make foreign counsel an important member of the litigation team.[1]

The types of assistance mentioned above that a lawyer seeks from local counsel in an interstate transaction would also be required from local counsel in an international transaction. In fact, the need for those types of assistance is greatly magnified when an international transaction is involved, since the likelihood of conflict between laws and practices of two or more countries is far greater than between two or more sister states. Moreover, other types of assistance should be sought from foreign local counsel that do not even suggest themselves when dealing with counsel in a sister state. These include help assessing political risks, differences in the regulatory and legal environment, and cultural and linguistic issues. Of course, implementation of a legal plan also will be far more difficult.

To fill these needs, the U.S. lawyer must carefully select and motivate foreign counsel. The U.S. lawyer also must fulfill a number of responsibilities implicitly owed to foreign counsel. The Southwestern Legal Foundation's multivolume series, *Private Investors Abroad,* contains numerous articles on dealing with foreign lawyers.

3. The U.S. Lawyer's Continuing Role

The U.S. lawyer will, of course, continue to participate in the international transaction in his or her customary role of advising on the laws of his or her home jurisdiction. However, because international transactions involve multiple national jurisdictions, the U.S. lawyer also must frequently serve as coordinator for the legal work in all jurisdictions. Otherwise, some crucial issues may remain hidden at great risk to the success of the matter.

a. Special U.S. Problems

The international nature of a transaction will bring into play numerous

---

1. *See* NANDA & PANSIUS, LITIGATION OF INTERNATIONAL DISPUTES IN U.S. COURTS (West Group 2000).

special U.S. federal and state laws that a lawyer involved primarily with a domestic practice seldom encounters. A small sampling of these special laws would include international trade laws, the Foreign Corrupt Practices Act, Anti-Boycott and Export Administration Regulations, Foreign Assets Control Regulations, International Financial and Investment Reporting Regulations, the U.S. taxation of foreign activities, and the Foreign Sovereign Immunities Act. In addition, domestic practitioners seldom encounter treaties and international conventions that often come into play in a transnational practice.

b. Special Foreign Problems

Realizing that his or her own jurisdiction has special rules affecting transnational matters, the U.S. lawyer should be alert to the possibility that other jurisdictions involved in an international transaction may have special rules as well. It is the U.S. lawyer's job to focus foreign local counsel's attention on that possibility, to help identify the applicable special rules, and to confirm that they are satisfactorily worked into the structure of the transaction.

c. Overall Responsibility

The U.S. lawyer might try to abdicate part of his or her responsibility by referring all non-U.S. legal matters ab initio to foreign counsel. However, the client would not normally be well served by that approach. No one would have an overall view of the legal aspects of the transaction. So, even though a U.S. lawyer may not be licensed to practice in any foreign jurisdictions, that lawyer cannot (figuratively, at least) leave his or her client at the water's edge.

The U.S. lawyer must attempt to ascertain applicable foreign law, not for purposes of giving a definitive opinion to the client on foreign law but (1) to guide foreign counsel effectively, (2) to seek creative methods of resolving any legal impasse that may arise during negotiations, and (3) to minimize the risk that some legal matters might be left untended or improperly analyzed (a situation that might occur if no lawyer took a transnational overview of the matter).

d. Procedure

The choice of structure for an international business or financial transaction will depend on considerations such as overall tax impact, practicality of structure (which is often necessary to establish a comfort factor among the parties), ease of administration, and local law requirements. After analyzing the tax and other legal ramifications of a particular activity in each relevant jurisdiction and the reasons behind local legal requirements, it is usually possible for counsel to create a structure that will mesh the local requirements of all jurisdictions involved without unduly hampering the overall business objectives. If this exercise is unsuccessful, the transaction probably should not be attempted.

I have found that devising an appropriate structure for a particular international operation requires an effective combination of imaginative planning by U.S. counsel and careful evaluation by foreign counsel. In determining the viability of a structure in a given jurisdiction, the best results are normally obtained by first preparing diagrams and memoranda from legal materials available in libraries here and on the Internet, then sending the diagrams and memoranda to foreign counsel for comment and approval in accordance with a suggested form of written opinion.

F. ENGAGEMENT OF FOREIGN COUNSEL

It is useful to develop a network of foreign legal correspondents, just like a bank develops a network of banking correspondents. In fact, one of the unique tools of an international lawyer is access to competent foreign legal counsel. And that tool is harder to acquire than you might think.

1. How to Find Them

It is easy to find lawyers in many foreign places, but it is never easy to find good ones. In some places it is even hard to find bad ones. Try finding a business lawyer in Libya right now. My most recent Libyan correspondent has moved to Miami.

a. Word-of-Mouth

Word-of-mouth is probably the best way to locate the right foreign counsel for your needs. Clients, adversaries, other foreign lawyers, and other U.S. lawyers can help. Keep a card or computer file of foreign lawyers you work with. Make a notation of each matter you work with them on. This will help you and others in the future.

The lawyer I correspond with most frequently in Panama came to my attention initially by referral from another Panamanian lawyer who could not assist with a particular matter due to a conflict of interest. I acquired my best Japanese correspondent after he capably represented the other side in a vessel financing. I once came into contact with a Luxembourg lawyer in a Euronote transaction whom I subsequently retained on a different transaction because I was impressed by his prompt and responsive assistance to his client, who had previously been my adversary.

b. Local Meetings

Another way to find foreign lawyers without leaving home is to attend internationally oriented symposia sponsored by bar associations, legal foundations, and law schools in the area. These events plus U.S. law school comparative law programs often attract ambitious, hard-working foreign lawyers who may be of great help to you when they return home.

c. International Associations

Membership in international lawyers' associations (such as the International Bar Association, the Union Internationale des Avocats, and the Inter-American Bar Association) is another useful means of cultivating these relationships. Many of those associations publish useful and fairly current directories of their members. They also sponsor conferences where acquaintances are established.

d. Directories and Other Publications

Failing some kind of direct or indirect personal connection, one can turn to the various directories of foreign lawyers that are available. The best use of directories, however, is not as an introduction but as a confirmation of an introduction made by some other means. For example, when I refer you to the law firm of Messrs. Argue & Phibbs in Sligo, Ireland, look it up in the Russell Law List. Current addresses and telecommunications information as well as useful biographical information often can be obtained in this manner.

Legal periodicals also are useful sources of foreign counsel. Of particular interest are the continuously appearing, somewhat gossipy articles on law firms that appear in Euromoney's *International Financial Law Review*. For example, articles have appeared there covering top Eurobond law firms, Spanish international law firms, and the elite Japanese firms.

G. WHAT TO LOOK FOR

1. The Ideal

The ideal foreign lawyer will respond to requests promptly, provide concise, accurate answers, and point out problem areas that you had perhaps overlooked. A good facilitator with both private and government parties in his jurisdiction, he or she will be sensitive to your concerns about the Foreign Corrupt Practices Act and local anti-bribery statutes. He or she will be apolitical but will know and be respected by the government officials who must be dealt with on your behalf. You do not want a dilettante (of which there are too many); you want a technician. Beware of lawyers who are really just promoters.

He or she will have word-processing and telecommunications equipment suitable for your work and a staff that is capable, responsible, and willing to work overtime.

2. The Reality

This ideal foreign lawyer does not exist; neither does the ideal U.S. lawyer. However, it is important for you to have formulated your own image of the ideal foreign lawyer so that you can size up likely candidates against your standard and make allowances in your planning to compensate for areas in which your chosen foreign counsel appears deficient.

3. Adjustments

For example, in many jurisdictions it will be difficult to find a lawyer who has any interest, much less ability, in tax matters. So you must compensate by relying more heavily on the opinions of nonlawyer accountants than might be the case in the United States. In fact, in some of the least-developed African countries the local accountant may be the only person who can give an informative view of any local laws, tax or otherwise. In those situations you are well-advised to retain a lawyer from the European nation that had the greatest colonial influence on the country in question. For example, many Paris lawyers specialize in commercial transactions with former French colonies. Their assistance can be invaluable (and in some cases the only reliable assistance available), even though technically they are not licensed to practice law in the former colony.

4. Regulation of Lawyers

In any case, care must be taken not to violate local laws regulating the activities of foreign lawyers. For example, foreign lawyers are permitted to work in Saudi Arabia. However, the foreign lawyer must be associated with a qualified Saudi national. All legal opinions must be signed by the Saudi national. Variations on this theme exist even in more sophisticated jurisdictions like England and many states in the United States.

H. HOW TO GET WHAT YOU NEED

Once you have found a foreign legal correspondent, how do you handle him or her? Diplomatically but firmly.

1. Ethics

Whatever else you do, do not (except in the special circumstances I will describe later) simply turn the matter over to your foreign lawyer and forget it, unless the matter and the client are of no concern to you. In fact, because of professional ethics you may find it essential to remain involved, especially if you are representing yourself as an international lawyer. In that case, your client should expect your continued "hands-on" attention to the matter. See the April 1984 issue of the newsletter for the State Bar of Texas, Section on International Law, which contains Mark Janis's article, "The Lawyer's Responsibility for Foreign Law and Foreign Lawyers,"[2] as well as Richard Graving's fine commentary on that article. These articles should be required reading for any lawyer who is ever involved with a transnational legal matter. More recent articles relating to international legal ethics and malpractice have appeared in publications dealing with malpractice loss prevention, such as the articles by Robert Creamer that appeared in the winter 1995 and fall 2000 issues of the ALAS *Loss Prevention Journal.*

2. Opinions

The U.S. and foreign lawyer's professional responsibility in international transactions is brought into focus particularly when formal legal opinions are involved. In obtaining an opinion from a foreign lawyer, it is important to make certain that he or she is fully aware of all your concerns. For example, remember to disclose to your Brazilian lawyer that your client intends to

---

2.   Janis's article was originally published at 16 INT'L LAW. 693 (1982).

discount the promissory note it is receiving from Petrobras (if such is the case). If you fail to cover that point, your Brazilian lawyer may not concern himself with whether the form of the note in the hands of an apparent holder in due course will be adequate to cut off personal defenses to the maker (that is, whether the note is truly a *negotiable* instrument).

I. WHAT YOU *CAN* TURN OVER TO FOREIGN COUNSEL

Obviously, there are some matters that can be completely turned over to competent foreign counsel because (1) there is no economic justification for participation by two lawyers, and the foreign lawyer can more readily and efficiently serve the client; (2) the matter is not really "international"; or (3) the client wants it that way. But these circumstances arise much less frequently than you might think.

J. WHAT YOU *CANNOT* TURN OVER TO FOREIGN COUNSEL

Several years ago a client I will call Joe contacted me about a new investment he wished to make in France. He already had some investments there and felt comfortable with the terrain. He preferred that I simply introduce him to a French lawyer, and he would take it from there. I did so, and contact was established between Joe and the French lawyer, whom I will call Jean.

1. Confronting Cultural Differences and Devising a Successful Plan

The first meeting was a disaster. Both spoke English and French, but culturally they were worlds apart. Joe called me from the Hotel Georges V totally frustrated. He had told Jean what he wanted to do and Jean had said it could not be done. Then Jean called me from his office equally frustrated. Joe, it seems, wanted to commit what was clearly an illegal act.

The true situation was somewhere in between. Joe had a goal that he had difficulty articulating. Instead, he described a plan that might have attained his goal but violated French exchange control laws of the time.

Jean was a well-respected *avocat à la cour* but was unaccustomed to consulting with clients in the planning stages of an investment. Most European clients do not use lawyers for business planning. So Jean did not know how to get Joe to clarify his goals and thus allow Jean to suggest alternative means of reaching those goals.

I made these observations by telephone to both Jean and Joe. After some discussion it was unanimously decided that I should attempt a proposal that Jean could approve. To do so, I researched relevant sources of French law available to me in Houston in light of my understanding of Joe's motivations and certain U.S. legal parameters. Then I discussed the plan with both gentlemen, fine-tuning it to incorporate their comments. Finally I faxed the plan to Paris. It worked!

It worked because Jean was a good lawyer and because I familiarized myself with the French legal issues involved sufficiently to ask him the right questions. The final work product became the joint effort of Yankee ingenuity (Texas-style) and French logic.

2. The Success of U.S. Lawyer Middlemen

American lawyers—culturally and educationally equipped as we are to be business planners—are uniquely qualified to serve as middlemen in such situations. This experience with Joe and Jean early in my career proved to me the value of American business lawyers as international middlemen. Without them, good deals frequently die; bad deals more often survive.

Vagts has stated this view most succinctly: "While an international lawyer need not be, indeed cannot be, a universal legal expert, he should at least be able to build bridges to foreign counsel and integrate their work with his. This is an art not developed by dealing with local counsel in Iowa."[3]

K. THE MECHANICS OF AN INTERNATIONAL LAW PRACTICE

1. Your Office

An international law office needs first-class telecommunications equipment and software. For example, at the last minute before the closing on a direct investment in Venezuela, a Venezuelan corporate entity was replaced by a Cayman Islands corporate entity, thus requiring a closing opinion on Cayman law. The Cayman lawyer justifiably insisted on seeing the documents, and one of the parties in New York insisted on seeing a manually signed facsimile of the Cayman opinion. The closing was accomplished on time (and timing was crucial) only because the proper hardware and software

---

3.   Vagts, *Are There No International Lawyers Anymore?* 75 AM. J. INT'L L. 134 at 135 (1981).

were available at both ends for the electronic transmission of the volumi-
nous documents (including signatures, thanks to fax machines and, even
better, optical scanners and digital cameras).

It also is important to have the proper word-processing typefaces for
frequently used foreign languages so that specialized letters of a foreign
alphabet, like the ñ in Spanish, can be utilized where appropriate. Think
how unprofessional the phrase "at two o'clock" would look if the apostro-
phe were omitted.

Your staff and your lawyers must not be afraid of foreign languages.
They might be able to avoid speaking them, but they must have the ingenuity to place and receive international telephone calls and leave intelligible
messages with their counterparts in other countries. They also must be
alert to the cultural sensitivities of foreign visitors to your office.

2. Your Library

A good international lawyer needs a good international law library. Unfortunately, the world is too big and the wallet too thin for a private law firm
to start with more than a very basic library. However, the Internet is a good
research tool. Additions to your library need only be made as necessary to
meet the demands of particular transactions as they arise. The precise slant
of your library will depend on the degree of concentration you undertake
for certain geographical areas or substantive subspecialties.

Once your interest in international law is noticed, you will be inundated with promotional materials by publishers in the field. Some of what
you see will be very good, but most of it will not be, so you must be very
selective. It seems that in many cases, the cost of a publication is inversely
proportional to the degree of its authority. Primary authorities such as statutes and regulations from foreign government sources are often available
at nominal cost (or e⸱   ᶜor free over the Internet), while secondary authorities written by unknown professors or practitioners often come only
at exorbitant cost.

3. Your Travel Schedule

Is constant face-to-face contact with foreign parties necessary? I don't think
so. This would involve too much travel for one or both parties. Generally,
international travel should be carefully limited. Although it may sound
inconsistent, a successful international lawyer does not have time to travel
except when it is absolutely essential.

Obviously, some trips cannot be avoided. You may need to attend a negotiating session in Oslo. You may find your presence at a closing in Santiago is essential, or you may need an eyeball-to-eyeball discussion with your local counsel in Jakarta on a crucial point of law in a very big deal. But I have discovered that I can practice international law, in most cases, far more effectively in my office than on a plane. Conversely, my foreign correspondents are more effective if they remain at home. The vast improvement in international telecommunications over the past few years has aided this approach.

There is a temptation to hop on a plane first and think about whether you really needed to after you are in the air. If you need to form a British Virgin Islands corporation, you can work out the terms of the memorandum and articles of association with your BVI correspondent by e-mail or fax and get the corporation formed in the course of a morning from your own desk. By doing so, you have saved at least two days of unnecessary travel time. Would you go to Delaware to form a Delaware corporation?

If you need a legal opinion from your French correspondent, you may be able to get it more promptly and just as reliably out of his or her New York office, providing you with the same service in a closer time zone or, if a face-to-face meeting is called for, with a shorter flight.

4. Your Foreign Office?

Do you need your own foreign offices? Not necessarily. A solid network of foreign correspondents may be sufficient and even better, since many foreign offices simply become high-overhead, loss-leading tourist bureaus. There are, or course, notable exceptions.

Providing legal services domestically and internationally is still usually a very personal, individualized activity, which permits the lawyer to serve the client out of a domestic office with lower costs and higher earnings. To the extent omnipresence is required, a good local correspondent or a fast plane can approximate that supernatural attribute far more efficiently than your own foreign office. Also, unless your practice is geographically constant, your foreign office is likely to be in the wrong place. Rather than having your own offices overseas, the better approach is normally "Have laptop, will travel."

5. Your Fees

Fee practices vary enormously from country to country, so it is good to treat the practices of a new foreign correspondent early either by means of open, frank discussion or requests for frequent billings to avoid surprises later. Most foreign lawyers involved with commercial transactions are willing to work for an agreed hourly rate, but some may protest, at least initially, that they are bound by statutory fee schedules based on a percentage of the value of the transaction. Even in jurisdictions where statutory fee schedules exist, there are normally exceptions for legal work that does not involve court appearances, conveyances, or administration of decedents' estates.

I once heard of a Houston company that was charged an inordinately high fee by a German lawyer for the review of a standby line of credit agreement. Unlike a standby *letter* of credit, this standby *line* of credit was clearly revocable at any time by the bank involved. In fact, the line was not really intended to be used at all other than as a safety valve for the benefit of the Houston company's German subsidiary in a very limited situation.

The German lawyer spent three hours reviewing and orally commenting on the agreement. By his own admission he did no other work, so you can imagine the chief financial officer's (CFO's) surprise when he received a bill for $12,000, or $4,000 per hour. The German lawyer's position was that his fee amounted to a very small percentage of the value of the transaction, assuming full utilization of the credit line over the entire term. After several fruitless telephone conversations between the CFO and the German lawyer, the company's Houston lawyer was called in to assist in reducing the fee, a cause in which the Houston lawyer was ultimately successful.

Two lessons can be learned from this experience. First and most obvious, fees should be discussed in advance. Second, if a problem arises, it is a problem that can best be resolved between lawyers. The U.S. lawyer can draw upon past and anticipated future good will that the foreign lawyer enjoys with the U.S. lawyer's firm. With that background, the two lawyers can more objectively discuss (1) the true expectations of both parties in terms of both fees and services, (2) a range of fair values for services performed in light of prevailing practices, and (3) in most cases an informal settlement that mollifies both parties, at least to the extent that an international incident is avoided.

Although encountered less frequently, some foreign lawyers charge too little. At first blush this would not seem to be a problem. However, if high-quality services are expected, you may find that the foreign lawyer is inadequately motivated by the low financial return. Then low fees cease to be a bargain.

In any event, the U.S. lawyer owes a duty to his foreign correspondent to see that the client promptly pays fees that the U.S. lawyer has approved. Refusals or an inability of a client to pay an approved fee must be handled very carefully on a case-by-case basis.

6. Identifying the Market

When I decided I wanted to practice international law, I despaired of finding a full-time practice in Houston. I thought that luxury was the special preserve of New York and Washington. I was pleased to find, therefore, a few lawyers doing it in Houston and doing it well.

That was in 1969. At the organizational meeting of the Houston Bar International Law Committee that year, five lawyers showed up. Thirty years later there are hundreds of lawyers in the Houston area who belong to what has now been institutionalized as the International Section of the Houston Bar Association. Yet if my practice is any indication, the supply of serious international lawyers still lags behind demand.

In Texas, the number of true international practitioners could be doubled and we would still be up to our necks in work. The reason is that as the Texas economy continues to grow and diversify, the number of lawyer-intensive international business opportunities and problems increases geometrically, and I expect this is the case in many other states as well. So far, the demand curve for international lawyers has been relatively free of downturns. New areas in which international lawyers may apply their expertise continue to appear just when older areas of activity begin to lag. For example, during some phases of an economic cycle, outbound investment and imports spur demand for international lawyers. During other phases, the focus will be on inbound investment and exports. Today, as new opportunities in less-developed countries arise, international lawyers will be focusing their energies in those directions.

In my view the future will remain bright. Like fast-food franchises, the more good international lawyers there are, the more clients will realize they need us. But you can only be successful if you find your proper niche in the market. Don't become an overnight expert on China, hire a Mandarin-speaking secretary, and expect the business to come rolling in—especially if the principal international business in your area is composed of agricultural exports to Europe. Be flexible.

Consider what international services your clients and potential clients really need. Study up on them and try your hand (within the limits of professional ethics, of course). Maybe there is a need for help with immigration or customs or export controls. Once you master these, you may choose to expand into other areas of the practice, depending on your interests and your clients' needs.

7. Attracting Clients

To attract clients, get out into the community and help build or add to the international infrastructure. Join and take a leadership role in international organizations like world trade associations, chambers of commerce, international business committees, or the IIE. If you perceive a need for an international organization that doesn't exist, organize one. Support legislation at the federal and state levels that encourages the international flow of trade and investment. These activities can serve as a form of institutional advertising for your interests and talents. As in any practice, of course, the best method of attracting new clients is to do your best for existing clients.

L. CONCLUSION

Recognizing that someone must assume a supervisory role over all legal aspects of an international transaction is the first priority to be grasped by the international lawyer. Thus, do your "homework" carefully. Familiarize yourself with relevant foreign laws and customs (the symphonic "score"), but also do some creative planning by considering alternatives for overcoming particular obstacles that you can expect to encounter at home and abroad. In addition, exercise care in the selection of foreign counsel. Finally, in dealing with foreign counsel, diplomacy and sensitivity are vital. Once mutual respect is established, the relationship with foreign counsel should bear fruit like the relationship between conductor and orchestra.

The role of the international lawyer as I have described it is not for everybody. To some it would not be glamorous enough. To some it may appear too glamorous. To others it would not be secure enough or would involve too much hard work. But it is a good, solid practice that, if properly handled, can prove to be extremely satisfying to the lawyer. The accomplished international lawyer can truly become the conductor of a global symphony.

Still In-house and Over Here

4

by Steven M. Glick

A. INTRODUCTION

Nearly a decade after my first contribution to *Careers in International Law* ("In House and Over Here: The Experience of a U.S. Attorney in an English Multinational Public Company"), I remain in-house and over here (London, England). I believe this provides reasonable evidence that a career in international law, even one spent largely outside the United States and outside private practice, is not only feasible but increasingly a normal career path for a U.S. lawyer. However, I remain convinced that when embarking on such a career, one should take certain steps to increase the prospect of success. There also are a few potential downsides to consider.

B. YOUR FIRST STEPS

1. Experience Private Practice

As someone who has worked in-house for over eight years and recruited many lawyers, I believe it is critical, in most cases, for young lawyers to spend four to six years in private practice before venturing in-house or overseas. Generally speaking, in-house law departments or small overseas offices of U.S. law firms cannot (or will not) give young lawyers the training or enable them to gain the quality and breadth of experience that they would receive in a medium-size or large law firm in the United States. What clients want the world over (whether in-house or private clients) is quality lawyering: technical and commercial expertise, transaction and interpersonal management skills, high levels of commitment and service, and the discretion and judgment that generally develop only after a few years in private practice.

In most cases, this expertise and skill is most easily obtained, and good habits formed, when you are working in your own language, within your own legal system, in an environment such as private practice that focuses extensively on the development of the lawyer. Overseas offices of U.S. firms or in-house law departments often are too small, or budgets too tight, to devote the appropriate amount of time and energy to this critical task.

2. Avoid Overspecialization

I also would recommend, if you know that you wish to practice in-house and/or overseas, that you try, to the extent possible, not to become overly specialized during your time in private practice. This is easier said than done, as the practice of law, particularly in the United States, becomes ever more specialized. If you must specialize, choose an area (for example, general corporate) that translates well into practicing overseas and is not particularly local by its very nature. Good corporate/commercial lawyers often can operate effectively in non-U.S. legal environments. There will clearly be less opportunity overseas for real estate lawyers, litigators, and probate lawyers. I became a corporate lawyer because I knew, at the outset of my career, that I wished to practice overseas and that I needed to choose a legal discipline that was transportable. Otherwise, I suspect I would have been a litigator.

3. Try Different Arenas

Try to gain, when in private practice, detailed exposure to a number of different industry/service markets. This may help you to decide what sort of in-house business might interest you. Undoubtedly, companies place a premium on lawyers who know the company's business, its products/services, and its markets; such knowledge also can enable the new in-house lawyer to "hit the ground running." This type of knowledge enables a lawyer to operate effectively and add value in a way that a "lay" lawyer often cannot. If you choose an industry and remain with it, you may become (or at least be perceived to be) even more valuable to your company, or marketable within other companies in that industry, because of the vast practical knowledge of doing business in that industry and the network of contacts developed over the years.

However, this industry knowledge can sometimes be overrated and a source of great inertia ("This is how we do it—we've always done it this way."). This is not perhaps a surprising view from someone who has moved from electronic instruments to leisure to entertainment. However, I believe companies indeed place a premium on market knowledge, even to the point that they are prepared to accept or tolerate less than first-class lawyering by someone familiar with the industry. They would not acknowledge or admit this, but I suspect it is sometimes the case.

4. Get Comfortable with the Numbers

Finally, understanding accounting, although not particularly from a technical standpoint, is of great importance. You need to understand a profit and loss statement and a balance sheet if you are going to speak the same language as many of your clients. You should be fluent in numbers. Early in my career I was told that I should read a prospectus or annual report from back to front, starting with the financials and ending with the narrative—good advice. When financial or tax matters are being discussed, don't tune out. Many of the opportunities to pursue a career as a lawyer in the international arena will require that you be comfortable with numbers, whether you are working in project finance, corporate finance, or mergers and acquisitions.

C. THREE WARNINGS

1. Know and Be Prepared for Clients' Expectations

There are many things you should consider as you embark on a career in international law. "As the world becomes smaller, expectations become greater," stated a recent marketing brochure for Denton Wilde Sapte, a major, London-based law firm with more than 800 lawyers and 35 offices in 23 countries. The brochure listed what clients need:

- Lawyers who are truly international
- Lawyers who know and understand your market
- Lawyers who are there for you
- Lawyers you can rely on
- Lawyers who can make things happen
- Lawyers who are available
- Lawyers who provide value for money
- Lawyers who share your goals

There may be nearly 1 million qualified U.S. lawyers, but few truly fit the bill that today's clients are demanding for their international work. When you embark on a career as an international lawyer, you enter, I believe, an even more demanding and exacting career than most overworked and overstressed lawyers are already experiencing.

A truly international practice from London means early-morning calls to deal with the Asia/Pacific region or calls late in the evening to deal with the West Coast (especially when the work is in the film industry, new media, or high-tech areas). It means frequent travel, often on weekends, and time away from home. For some, this is the appeal; for others, this may be a major disadvantage. If you speak foreign languages, you will have an opportunity to use them, but if you do not, doing business can sometimes become protracted with interpreters, translators, and so on. You need to be expert in certain areas of "domestic law," but you also need to understand local laws, customs and practices, and business conditions in many other countries.

2. Know the Enemy Within . . .

If you end up in-house, there are two things that may be of concern: the enemy within and the enemy without. After my eight years in private practice, the political and divisive nature of a company came as a disappointment to me when I became in-house general counsel. And at the senior levels, the political game can become more important. Having grown up in a professional environment, I have not fully adapted to this situation, and it may yet, one day, cause me to leave the in-house practice of law.

3. . . . and Without

The enemy without is perhaps the phenomenon of the last 20 years. With the seemingly unending spate of mergers, acquisitions, de-mergers, restructurings, and downsizings, there are really very few positions where an in-house lawyer can be insulated from these changes. Within six months of my leaving my first in-house position as business and legal affairs director of Graseby plc, the company was acquired by Smiths Industries and my successor, as well as all of my former board colleagues, left the company. Within one year of my departure from my second in-house job as general counsel of Hilton Group plc (the $6 billion Hilton hotel and betting and gaming group), the chief executive of the group and the two division managing directors, among others, were gone and the Legal Department was subsequently restructured with job losses. Finally and perhaps most illustrative, between my acceptance of the offer for my current position and the time I started, Universal Studios, one of the company's two shareholders, announced that after 20 years it wished to terminate the joint venture (known as CIC Video International). Several months later, Paramount Pictures, the other original shareholder, wholly owned a company whose headcount had to be reduced significantly to accommodate an even larger reduction in revenues caused by the loss of Universal products.

Change is all around you when you are in-house, and if it is not the next hostile bidder or the next change in management that creates internal upheaval, it could be market conditions, technological obsolescence, or one of many other risk factors. Partnership in or an affiliation with a law firm can thus seem to be a pillar of stability compared to an in-house practice that can and does suffer many disruptions. Few in-house lawyers lose sleep (at least for too long) over this situation, as it has become a way of life. Further, despite Shakespeare's oft-quoted line "let's kill all the lawyers," lawyers are not usually the first to go in a period of corporate change, because they are needed, at least initially, to implement the change.

D. CONCLUSION

I have now spent eight years in private practice and eight years in-house, mostly involved in cross-border or international matters. It has been hard work, harder than I ever imagined or actually sought. It also has generally been challenging, so much so that I often fantasize about a less intellectually rigorous career. And at times it has been frustrating and even disappointing. But the people I have met and the places I have been and the things I have done make it all worthwhile. I have never really longed to hang up the general practice shingle on the village green, unless it happens to be on the moon. Let's save that for my third and final contribution, in, say, ten years' time, to the ABA's *Careers in Inter-Galactic Law.*

A Career in International Commercial Arbitration

5

by Marc J. Goldstein

A. INTRODUCTION

The proper path in life often is learned by not following it. So it was for me, in my career in international litigation and arbitration. I went to law school determined to become a fire-breathing courtroom lawyer. Take a specialized class in international dispute resolution? This seemed a distant and irrelevant body of knowledge. Today I would urge all aspiring litigators, and even aspiring corporate lawyers, to take that course, because application of the principal international agreements on arbitration will probably be unavoidable in life as a lawyer. A working knowledge of these treaties on the enforcement of arbitration agreements and awards, and how those treaties are enforced in the courts of the United States, is essential working knowledge, part of the litigator's working vocabulary in the same sense as the Federal Rules of Civil Procedure. The same may be said for the arbitration rules of the leading international arbitration institutions (International Chamber of Commerce [ICC], American Arbitration Association [AAA], London Court of International Arbitration, and various institutional rules based upon the United Nations Commission on International Trade Law [UNCITRAL] Rules).

Similarly, after following the linear path from law school to a large New York City law firm, I only discovered through contacts with others undreamt-of career possibilities: clerkships with international tribunals; study programs in comparative law and civil law at foreign law schools; counsel positions with major international arbitral institutions; apprenticeships with foreign law firms; and associate positions in foreign offices of U.S. law firms.

B. FROM NEW YORK TO THE HAGUE

My own introduction to international arbitration was involuntary: I was drafted, as a young associate, from a budding career as an antitrust and securities litigator to devote most of my time to a complex expropriation case before the Iran-U.S. Claims Tribunal in The Hague. This was not necessarily considered a plum assignment for an associate in the mid-1980s, a few years before "globalization" became a hot item in the legal profession. I spent nearly four years in a state of deep ambivalence. While my peers were taking and defending depositions, and even trying cases before juries in state and federal courts, I was learning the complexities of the valuation of nationalized property in international law, the discounted cash-flow method, principles of accounting for real estate development projects, and more about the construction industry than I would ever have cared to know. But I also was learning important lessons—although I perhaps did not realize it at the time—about cross-cultural communications in the legal profession, evidence in international tribunals, and how jurists from different legal cultures can evaluate the same set of facts in dramatically different ways.

Along the way, of course, I also had personal experiences that peers did not share: roasted reindeer in Malmo, Sweden; swimming in the North Sea; hearings in the Czar Nicholas room of the Peace Palace in The Hague. And I had my first exposure to the courtesy culture of international arbitration: the numerous shared meals, coffee breaks, and cocktails that surrounded the proceedings and brought lawyers into contact with arbitrators in ways that are unheard of in bench-bar relations in the United States.

1. International Arbitration Literature

My experience at the Iran-U.S. Claims Tribunal also exposed me to an important dimension of international arbitration—its vast literature. This was a field where professors acted as lawyers, lawyers wrote for publication as if they were professors, and the line between academia and practice was blurred in the ranks of arbitrators and counsel. Moreover, this was a field where active practitioners kept up with the literature. Because of the tradition of confidentiality of arbitration proceedings, the scholarly literature in the field assumes a special importance for the exchange of ideas. The lesson for a career-building young practitioner in this field was clear: publication could be a most worthwhile activity, a way to make an impact and contribute to one's reputation in the field in an effective way.

C. CHOOSING A LAW FIRM

Good advice to the aspiring lawyer in this field also includes suggestions on the choice of a law firm. In a sense such advice does not differ very much from what one would say about any specialized field: join a firm with an established practice. But in the field of international dispute resolution, some special considerations may apply. First: join a firm with a large and established practice in international commercial transactions. International arbitrations originate in contracts; parties to contracts often are loyal and continuing clients of the lawyers who drafted the contracts for them. One of my earliest international commercial arbitrations, after my experience in the Iran-U.S. Claims Tribunal, was for a U.S. company that had been a client of my firm for more than three decades. The contract containing the arbitration clause had been signed in 1979; the dispute arose in 1990. The client was loyal, and called us immediately.

A second suggestion is to join a firm where you will have the privilege to work as an apprentice to one of the world's leading international arbitrators. International arbitration remains one of the most exclusive professional "clubs" in the world, and even the new practitioner identifies its members relatively easily.[1] In large international commercial arbitrations, it is usually the privilege of the presiding arbitrator to select an associate to act as law secretary to the Tribunal—the equivalent of a judicial law clerk—who studies the parties' memorials, evaluates the evidence, researches the legal questions, and drafts orders and awards.

Once you have found a place in this specialty, build your career by being a writer and a joiner. Identify the major publications followed by the

---

1.   See, for example, the membership list of the International Council on Commercial Arbitration (ICCA), which can be found in the annual ICCA YEARBOOK ON COMMERCIAL ARBITRATION. This is not an exhaustive list, but it is certainly a good start. For a more extensive list of U.S. practitioners, you might subscribe to the newsletters of the Institute for Transnational Arbitration or the ABA Section of International Law and Practice's International Commercial Arbitration Committee.

international arbitration bar around the world and find time to contribute articles to them.[2] Be a member of the interational arbitration or international litigation committee of your local bar association. Join the ABA Section of International Law and Practice and become active in its International Commercial Arbitration Committee. Consider membership in the Institute for Transnational Arbitration, the Corporate Counsel Committee of the American Arbitration Association, and the American Society of International Law. Participate in one of the Fellowship courses offered by the United Kingdom's Chartered Institute of Arbitrators, and become a Fellow by passing the Fellowship examination. Attend the meetings of the organizations you join, and become a friend and colleague of fellow practitioners around the world.

Further, make your interest and talent in the field known to your colleagues in the firm. Be the first litigator on your floor to master the main legal research sources used by international arbitration practitioners. Once you have learned to navigate the annual *Yearbook of the International Council on Commercial Arbitration* (ICCA), the ICCA Congress Series, the *ICC Bulletin*, and several of the more significant Web sites that track developments in international commercial arbitration (for example, <www.internationaladr.com>), you will have made yourself marketable to the more senior practitioners in your firm.

D. THE REWARDS OF A CAREER IN INTERNATIONAL COMMERCIAL ARBITRATION

What might be the rewards of a career in the practice of international commercial arbitration? I approach this question with a particular viewpoint, having gradually shifted my practice from one that was predominantly litigation in the state and federal courts to one that is predominantly before international arbitral tribunals.

First, I have found that presenting the case to an arbitral tribunal composed entirely, or substantially, of arbitrators selected by the parties is an intellectually and personally gratifying experience. In some state court systems in the United States, the commercial judges often come to the bench from careers in criminal courts or other civil courts, and infrequently have the experience or enthusiasm for the complex issues that international liti-

---

2.   A short list would include the JOURNAL OF INTERNATIONAL ARBITRATION, ARBITRATION INTERNATIONAL, AMERICAN REVIEW OF INTERNATIONAL ARBITRATION, MEALEY'S INTERNATIONAL ARBITRATION REPORT, and the INTERNATIONAL CHAMBER OF COMMERCE BULLETIN.

gations often present. These are courts of general jurisdiction, crowded with cases of all stripes, but mainly with cases that involve disputes among local individuals, companies, and governments. The judges often are elected officials, and their level of dedication to legal scholarship will vary widely. The quality of adjudication will generally be better in the federal courts, but if one views the U.S. model of litigation with its emphasis on pretrial discovery as a flawed model, then it is easy to develop an affection for the international arbitration process.

1. Discovery American-Style

This is not the occasion to debate whether discovery American-style does or does not surpass the more hybrid civil law–common law model of evidence-gathering that prevails in international commercial arbitration. This chapter focuses on career selection, and accordingly the young practitioner may wish to consider a reality of the litigation world that is not often mentioned in job interviews. The U.S. adversary system remains a bruising, fractious, confrontational, and frequently discourteous and even vicious process for resolving disputes. Moreover, the discovery process often brings out the worst characteristics of practitioners, as they are to a large extent left without direct judicial supervision to conduct hand-to-hand combat in pretrial exchanges of documents and in depositions. U.S. litigation is not a field for the weak of heart, and many young lawyers who are attracted by the intellectual dimension of litigation ultimately make career decisions against the field precisely because of the inherent unpleasantness of it.

2. Discovery in International Commercial Arbitration

In international commercial arbitration, unlike U.S. litigation, there is relatively little occasion for the parties' lawyers to communicate with one another except through the medium of their respective communications to the arbitral tribunal. Any request for discovery must be addressed to the arbitral tribunal. Any objection to discovery must be addressed to the arbitral tribunal. Indeed, there is scarcely any form of procedural or substantive relief that a party would seek in international arbitration that would involve, to any significant degree, communications *inter se* among counsel without involvement of the Arbitral Tribunal. The result of this process, in my experience, is an elevated level of rhetoric and argument, and less hyperbole, overstatement, misstatement, and ad hominem attacks on opposing counsel.

The result is that the most intensely contested matters, even those involving international political animosity as well as divergent economic positions, can proceed in an environment of utmost courtesy and mutual respect.

3. The Quality of Arbitrators

Further, the arbitral tribunal has been engaged by the parties and/or the arbitral institution specifically to fulfill a mission in this particular case. The arbitrators are not civil servants, nor do they enjoy the lifetime tenure of federal judges in the United States. If a complex case requires extensive written submissions from the parties or an extended number of days or weeks for evidentiary hearings, it is more likely that an international arbitral tribunal, as compared to a domestic court, will devote the time and attention that the matter requires. The arbitrators, for one thing, are compensated for their time. Further, while arbitrators also are busy practitioners with heavy caseloads, their work is conducted under a microscope in ways that the work of domestic judges is not. Since the careers of international arbitrators depend on their reputations, they want to impress one another, the counsel and parties who appear before them, and the arbitral institutions that appointed them—and, particularly in the case of ICC arbitration, have the opportunity to review the arbitrators' awards before they are issued. These factors do not necessarily ensure a better quality of justice than that dispensed in the domestic litigation system, but they do create momentum favoring a high level of scholarship and rigorous analysis in international arbitration awards.

Why should this be a factor of significance in a fledgling lawyer's career selection? The answer is that, unfortunately, economic realities and human frailties limit the quality of justice dispensed by courts. As a litigator in a complex case, you devote tireless effort to the effective presentation of evidence, argument, and authority in support of your client's position. You want to win, of course. But you also want to see your work product treated with the respect it deserves by the decision makers. So does your client, who has paid tens or hundreds of thousands of dollars for your efforts. You want your arguments, and those of the other side, addressed in a thoughtful and intellectually honest way, in decisions that are carefully and systematically reasoned, and uninfected by the personal bias of the jurist. Since winning and losing cannot be the only measure of your professional satisfaction, you at some point realize that much of your satisfaction is derived from having a jurist or arbitrators who treat the issues and authorities with the same passionate attention that you do. The truth, in this practitioner's experience—unfortunate truth, in the sense that it is a negative commentary on the U.S. judicial system—is that international arbitrators behave in this fashion more often than do U.S. judges. Anyone who reads the international arbitration awards that are published in the *Mealey's International Arbitration Report* cannot help but be struck by the precision with which arbitrators present the contentions of the parties, the care with which they formulate the issues presented for decision, and the comprehensiveness of their analysis and citation of relevant authority.

4. Other Attractions

Other aspects of the international arbitration process also may be attractive to the young lawyer who is attracted to dispute resolution practice, but leery of the time demands and stress often said to be associated with litigation practice in large U.S. law firms. First, the limitations on discovery in international arbitration substantially eliminate much of the tedium associated with the production of documents and the preparation of responses to interrogatories, tasks that unfortunately but necessarily are assigned to the most junior lawyers on the team in a U.S. litigation. I often cringe at the notion that young lawyers are receiving any "training" when they are called upon to review hundreds of thousands of documents from a client's files for attorney-client privilege in advance of their production, or to wade through a similar volume of documents produced by an adverse party, or to spend grueling days reviewing the fruits of document discovery from multiple parties and nonparties in a central document "repository." There is document discovery in international arbitration, within limitations imposed on a case-by-case basis by the arbitrators. But the influence of civil law systems on the process has made it next to impossible for counsel to successfully request and obtain "all documents referring or relating to" a particular issue or contention. Thus, not only is the production of useless mounds of documents eliminated, but also much of the squabbling among lawyers about whether particular discovery requests are unduly burdensome, and whether the adverse party by objecting is seeking to conceal information germane to the case.

Further, in most international arbitrations the arbitrators have no effective powers to compel production of documents or other discovery from noncombatants, that is, third parties (except in the rare instance where such parties are domiciled at the place of arbitration, in which case such assistance might be obtained through a local court). This dramatically reduces the scope of potential discovery, as compared to domestic litigation. The result is that international arbitration is rather more directly channeled to the heart of the matter. And, for the young lawyer, there is the opportunity to be closely involved in shaping the client's litigation strategy, drafting the pleadings, and working with the most significant documentary evidence from your own client's files rather than being preoccupied with the detective work that prevails in U.S. litigation, as adverse parties send teams of young lawyers on the often fruitless quest for the "smoking gun" in the other party's files.

Another "lifestyle" issue is the pace of the action. International arbitration is a tightly controlled process in which the arbitral tribunal determines what submissions each party will be permitted to make and when they will be made. The result is that, while work on an international arbitration case certainly can be as intense and time-consuming as any other work in dispute resolution practice, it does tend to follow a relatively stable pattern of "my turn, your turn." The claimant submits its Statement of Claim, the respondent submits its Answer/Statement of Defense. The claimant submits an application for interim measures of protection, the respondent submits an opposition to the application. Generally such submissions are made pursuant to a procedural timetable fixed in advance by the arbitral tribunal. This contrasts with the crazy-quilt pattern of domestic litigation in the United States, in which motions often can be made at any time and without prior permission of the court, and counsel are likely to be confronted with several motions—many of them, unfortunately, relating to discovery—at any one time. Do not plan your weekends far in advance!

5. Over the Long Term

The young lawyer also may wish to consider the longer-term rewards of a specialization in international commercial arbitration. International arbitration practice is no more remunerative than any other specialization within the private practice of law. But I believe the nonmonetary rewards of such a practice are considerable, at least when compared to domestic dispute resolution practice. Significantly, you are joining a truly global association of professionals in this field who have defined themselves, through various organizations and associations, formal and informal, as the "international arbitration bar." Each time you appear as counsel in a case, there is a new opportunity to expand your professional reputation through the impression you make on opposing counsel, and on each of the three members of the arbitral tribunal, each of whom is likely to be a private practitioner whose impressions of your work will add luster to your global reputation. By the time you have acted as counsel in your tenth international arbitration, you will have appeared before 30 international arbitrators from all corners of the globe, done battle with many of the best law firms in the world, engaged and worked with co-counsel and experts who are themselves among the foremost practitioners in the field—and your own reputation should indeed be global! Add to this your participation in conferences on international arbitration, your contributions to publications, and your own service as an arbitrator and as a member of various committees and associations, and you should have the opportunity to develop the kind of extensive network of personal and professional contacts that is, in a sense, its own reward (not to mention a source of referrals that should help you to build a substantial practice).

E. ADVICE ON CAREER PREPARATION

What, then, are the specific career initiatives that the aspiring international arbitration practitioner should take, beginning in law school and going forward? Here is a nonexhaustive list:

- *Consider obtaining an advanced law degree in international law and/ or comparative law from a law school outside the United States*, and at the same time perfecting your skills in a second language. International arbitration procedures are an amalgam of common law and civil law procedures, and often they are applied by arbitral tribunals in which common law and civil law traditions are each represented. Further, your ability to be an effective advocate for your clients in international arbitration will ultimately depend on your ability to communicate effectively with arbitrators from different legal and cultural traditions. Accordingly, training to be a comparativist at an early stage of your career will stand you in good stead later on.

- *Do not pass up the opportunities, if they are available to you, to serve in judicial clerkship positions within the U.S. federal system.* Bear in mind that, later on in your career, when you are being evaluated as a potential counsel in an international arbitration case, clients, foreign and American, will want to assess quickly your pedigree as an American trial lawyer. For the same reason, if you have an opportunity to serve in a prosecuting position in a U.S. attorney's office, seize it.

- *Seek a governmental or judicial position specifically involved with international law or international dispute resolution.* A clerkship on an international arbitral tribunal such as the Iran-U.S. Claims Tribunal is one example. Serving in the Office of the Legal Adviser in the U.S. Department of State is another. Opportunities for up-close exposure to international dispute resolution also exist within a variety of international organizations, including United Nations–related organizations such as the Geneva-based World Intellectual Property Organization (WIPO), which sponsors international arbitrations, and the Vienna-based United Nations Commission on International Trade Law (UNCITRAL), which is among the most active organizations in the world in the study of policy issues relating to international arbitration. You also may wish to consider service as staff counsel at the International Chamber of Commerce (ICC) International Court of Arbitration, based in Paris, which remains the world's most active institutional administrator of international arbitrations. Counsel at the ICC Secretariat are generally young lawyers with an interest in international arbitration. These positions are essentially apprenticeship positions with heavy administrative responsibility, but they offer the opportunity to participate in the selection of arbitrators and in the important work of the ICC Court in the management of ICC arbitrations.

- *Consider beginning your career in private practice in a foreign office of a U.S. law firm, or the office of a foreign law firm, which has an extensive specialized practice in international arbitration*, and in particular is the home to one or more practitioners who frequently serve as presiding arbitrators in complex international commercial arbitrations. Working with such a mentor, you will have an opportunity equivalent to that of a judicial law clerk in the U.S. system, to master the facts, evidence, and applicable law; research the legal issues; and participate in the drafting of awards. With the same mentor, you are likely to serve as co-counsel in challenging, complex international arbitration cases; assist in preparing articles for publication; and appear as a speaker in international conferences on international commercial arbitration.

- *Be a "joiner" early in your career,* volunteering your time and effort to various professional associations (in exchange, implicitly, for exposure of your name and your talent). Be involved in the international arbitration committee of the ABA Section of International Law and Practice. Seek membership in the Institute for Transnational Arbitration, and attend its annual conference. Certainly join the international arbitration committees of your local and state bar associations. Become a member of the International Bar Association, and in particular its Committee D, which focuses on international dispute resolution. Seek to become a Fellow of the Chartered Institute of Arbitrators, which is based in the United Kingdom and has branches in North America and generally throughout the British Commonwealth. The Chartered Institute offers "fast-track" fellowship courses for experienced professionals, which are generally intensive sessions over a period of several days, including oral evaluation and written examination.

- *Do superb legal work.* The international arbitration bar is a fluid and highly interconnected worldwide network. Particularly because members of this community are constantly in touch with one another concerning the selection of arbitrators, experts, and counsel, this is uniquely a branch of the bar in which the participants are undergoing constant and intensive peer evaluation. This may seem like advice to do things the old-fashioned way, but it remains true that the essential element of your long-range business development plan is your reputation for excellence.

- *Read the literature in the field on a regular basis.* You should subscribe to the *ICCA Yearbook*, the *Journal of International Arbitration, Arbitration International, Mealey's International Arbitration Report,* the *ICC Bulletin*, and the *American Review of International Arbitration.* Find a number of Web sites that focus on international arbitration, and know how to navigate them to find rules, analyses, and bibliographies. Useful sites include those maintained by major international arbitration institutions such as the WIPO, the ICC, and the LCIA, <www.internationaladr.com>, and sites of major publishing houses in the field, such as Kluwer Law Publishing.

- *Seek to have your name included in the lists of arbitrators of major international arbitration institutions*: the AAA, ICC, LCIA, WIPO,

Stockholm Chamber of Commerce, Hong Kong International Arbitration Center, Singapore International Arbitration Center, and the British Columbia International Arbitration Center. Eventually, opportunities for service as an arbitrator will begin to come your way. You can cross-fertilize your practice as counsel and as arbitrator. Each should nourish the other.

F.   WHERE THE ROAD LEADS

So where might you find yourself after 20 years in practice, if you follow the sage advice given above? I cannot precisely tell you because, as I stated at the outset, I was a latecomer to the world of international commercial arbitration. But I have had the good fortune to intervene as counsel in several very complex, very high-stakes, very high-profile international commercial arbitrations. I have had the privilege of pleading on behalf of my clients before some of the most illustrious international arbitrators in the world. I presently have international commercial arbitrations pending on three continents, none of which is North America. I represent clients from Europe, North America, and South America. I travel extensively and divide my time between the New York and Paris offices of my firm. I have had the privilege of working in close collaboration with expert witnesses of foreign and international law who have truly extraordinary legal minds and also are genuinely outstanding people. I have a network of friends and professional contacts that nearly spans the globe—and, with the benefit of e-mail, the ability to keep up with them on a daily basis.

If the definition of success in life is to be able to earn a livelihood doing work from which one derives great pleasure, then I can claim a measure of success.

From New York to Madrid via Paris: Smaller Pond, Bigger Fish?

6

by Clifford J. Hendel

A. INTRODUCTION

I had an inclination toward an international career before I entered law school. As an undergraduate, I spent a semester in Madrid. After college, I considered careers with the Department of State and even was offered a job as an economic analyst with the C.I.A., but since this was during the Iran hostage crisis, these careers seemed a bit risky. So, after a year or so as a management consultant in an accounting firm's consultancy division and some time working on a state political campaign, I opted for law school instead.

In law school, I had the opportunity to spend a semester at the University of Exeter in England, where I learned the basic elements of European Economic Community law and studied some comparative law that I could not have obtained in the United States, as well as a little French and German.

B. WHAT IS MY JOB?

I now practice in Madrid as a partner of a small but growing "boutique" firm (which the local business press has characterized as one of the "jewels in the crown" of the Spanish profession) whose practice in large part is oriented toward high-visibility mergers and acquisitions (M&A) and related work. Our firm currently has 13 lawyers; I am the only non-Spaniard.

My work involves two broad categories: Spanish and international.

The first category includes the range of work that clients bring to our firm involving Spanish investments and operations. A few examples in this area include: advising a leading U.K. chain of fitness clubs in its expansion into the Spanish market; a Scandinavian telecommunications operator as member of a consortium that was awarded a license for provision of "third-generation" mobile telephone services in Spain and as prospective purchaser of one of Spain's leading Internet portals; and a major U.S.-based Internet advertising company in the termination of a joint venture with a leading Spanish telecoms entity and the expansion of its activities in Spain. Although I refer to these matters as Spanish, they generally include important international elements; for example, the clients are frequently from other countries, and the structure or underlying "mind-set" of the transaction often reflects international practices. Thus, the clients' experience and expectations may need certain massaging or explaining in order to achieve their desired objectives in the legal/commercial context of Spain with which they may be unfamiliar, and my background and experience qualifies me to help them.

My international assignments sometimes do not have a significant nexus to Spain or Spanish law, but for a variety of reasons may reach my desk nonetheless. The nature and quantity of these matters vary—in the past year or so perhaps involving 25 to 30 percent of my time, and in peak periods at or even above 50 percent. These sorts of matters include advising a French/Swiss bottled-water giant in the establishment of a joint venture and expansion in Latin America and, subsequently, in a series of acquisitions in various regions of the globe, including Eastern Europe and the Middle East; counseling a Brazilian electrical equipment manufacturer in an international arbitration—an area that we have identified as poised for great growth in Spain and Latin America—arising out of claims from an African construction project; and advising a French bank in various international aircraft lease financings. In these matters, there is no need for me to burden my Spanish colleagues with requests for assistance.

Occasionally, my work involves matters that are hybrids and are not fairly characterized as either Spanish or international. For example, I recently advised a Spanish manufacturer and distributor of fitness equipment in connection with the possible acquisition of a U.S.-based manufacturer and distributor of complementary equipment and the possible acquisition of certain European distribution rights from an unrelated entity in the same sector. This was done with an eye to creating a global leader in the sector.

C. HOW DID I GET TO WHERE I AM?

Upon graduation from law school at a fine but "regional" East Coast institution, I had a strong desire to do something international, and so tried to find a position with a New York firm. At the time, however, New York firms had little interest in applicants from schools that were slightly off their mainstream radar screen, particularly applicants like me whose law school grades were somewhat less than stellar. So when graduation rolled around, I had not yet found a job.

But I got lucky. A new federal district court judgeship had been created in the district in which I lived and the Senate had cleared the candidate. I applied for the two-year clerkship position and got the job. For the next two years, I observed and participated in the processing and resolution of a broad range of civil and criminal matters alongside an extremely energetic, capable, and conscientious judge. As my clerkship drew to an end, I found that the position seemed to have added enough luster to my curriculum vitae to compensate for the perceived deficiencies that had prevented me from finding a suitable position with a New York firm two years before. My choice now was between white-collar criminal work in a (now-defunct) large domestic New York firm with a prominent lawyer who is now a distinguished federal district court judge in Manhattan, and one of the most internationally active of the New York–based firms, where I could join, after a period of rotation, any department that I desired. I accepted the latter position, and, after an interesting several months in the newly created international arbitration department of the firm, decided that my international interests—still principally oriented toward Latin America and Spain—would be better served in the corporate department of the firm.

I rather quickly became specialized in asset-financing transactions, particularly involving aircraft leveraged leasing. While many of these transactions were purely domestic, a number were structured as cross-border or "double-dip" leases, in which the differing treatment for tax and/or commercial law purposes of the same transaction under different legal systems could be used to the advantage of the parties. Still, for some years I had significant trouble getting the attention of the lawyers at the firm who dealt with Latin or Spanish matters, and found myself increasingly specialized in the asset finance practice area, where I developed the drafting, structuring, and negotiating skills that have been my key professional assets ever since.

I also had a chance to serve one night a month as arbitrator/judge in New York City's Small Claims Court.

Then I had another stroke of luck. One of the firm's Argentine clients sold a New York banking affiliate to a leading Spanish bank, and the Spaniards asked us to continue representing the affiliate. Another Spanish bank asked for help in arranging various secured and unsecured financings for their U.S. clients out of their New York branch. I began to work closely with the partner responsible for these two client relationships and to develop good relationships of my own with these clients. When a transaction arose involving the restructuring of the debt owed by a Central American country to the Pentagon, I found myself advising the central bank and the finance ministry of the country in question in their capital city. Thus, after several years of practice, I now had an asset finance "hat" and a Spanish/ Latin client "hat" to wear at the firm.

These incipient relationships with Spanish banks came at a time when the firm was in a period of global expansion. Thus, the firm proposed that I spend a year or so at a Spanish firm on "loan" or "secondment" to acquaint myself with the Spanish market and foster my relationship with our existing Spanish clients. I found and arranged a secondment with one of the leading Spanish firms, one of whose associates was at the time a foreign associate at a competing major New York firm, and, with full support and subsidization from the home office, crossed the Atlantic for what I expected to be a year-long tour of duty in late 1991.

I then spent slightly over a year with a fine Spanish firm, reinventing myself to some extent as an M&A lawyer, as that was the bread-and-butter area of practice at the time in Spain and one of the strongest areas of the Spanish firm's practice. During my stay in Spain, I realized that I was actually a more complete and well-rounded lawyer than I had thought myself to be in New York, that my New York–acquired skills in negotiating and particularly in drafting would be very useful anywhere, and that my level of Spanish was actually quite a bit higher than I had thought. All of these factors contributed to making the secondment a big success, not only for me personally but for my New York firm and the Spanish firm as well.

But the secondment almost came to a premature end when I was assisting one of the New York firm's Spanish bank clients in a public offering of debt in the United States and a controversy arose between the bank and its largest shareholder, a client of the Spanish firm. This controversy placed me in a very awkward position. My access to information obtained from the Spanish firm's representation of the shareholder was, or could have been, material to the investors in the public offering but the bank may not have been aware of it or at least may not have made its advisors aware in the course of the due diligence carried out in connection with the offering. Fortunately, this particular quandary resolved itself amicably between the parties, but it was clear that I could not continue to work indefinitely for two firms at the same time: the possibility of conflict was too great.

As the secondment drew to a close, another dilemma arose: what to do with our firm's expanding relations with Spain and Spanish clients, and in particular, what to do with me. If I returned to New York, according to the original plan, there was a substantial risk that the relations that I had nurtured would grow cold. On the other hand, there was not a suitable way to keep me in Spain—the firm did not wish to open a Madrid office. This conundrum was solved in a way that, in hindsight, probably represents the greatest stroke of luck that I have had in my career: the New York firm proposed that I relocate to the firm's long-established and short-staffed Paris office, from which I could continue to be in close touch with our Spanish clients and developments in Spain generally.

Thus, in late 1992, with virtually no French-language ability and only the vaguest ideas about French history and culture, I moved to Paris, expecting that this would be a mere prelude to an early return to Spain in some fashion with the New York firm. However, the Spanish front did not develop as quickly or as promisingly as expected, so no imminent, triumphal return to Spain was in the cards. At the same time, my posting in Paris was proving to be fortuitous and quite successful. The French-based asset and project finance market was booming, my New York experience in this area was a great asset, and my experience in private European M&A transactions also was very useful in many transactions. In short, in Paris there was a large and growing market for internationally oriented, financially trained lawyers, and we U.S.-trained financial lawyers were nicely positioned to exploit the opportunities presented.

Time passed, my French reached acceptable levels, and I began to think of making Paris my permanent base, or of ways to arrange a split Paris/ Madrid base. For a variety of reasons, the Spanish venture did not take wing. But I was becoming more and more settled in Paris, and more and more convinced that I would likely spend many more years in Europe.

This fact caused me to think seriously about the question of becoming admitted to practice locally. Unfortunately, at the time, the previously hospitable French rules on admission to practice of foreign lawyers had been recently and radically tightened; my timid inquiries of the Paris and French national bar authorities as to the rules and procedures for my becoming admitted under the new regime were met with such a glacial response that I quickly dropped the issue. But, since the English rules had just been greatly liberalized and were as transparent and "foreigner-friendly" as the French rules were opaque and xenophobic, I decided to prepare for the "Qualified Lawyers Transfer Test," a kind of mini–bar exam required for admission by foreign lawyers (or barristers) as an English solicitor.

I passed the exam in 1995 and became admitted as a solicitor. Shortly afterwards, I learned of a possible interpretation of the French rules by the Paris bar authorities that might permit me to become admitted as an *avocat*. Since this admission would have certain practical consequences for me— the firm had advised me that it would be probably unlawful and in any event too risky to name me a partner based in Paris when I was not locally admitted, and I had agreed to a promotion to "of counsel" pending my eventual admission—I pursued it as well. At the same time, and notwithstanding my professional success and prospects in Paris, personal reasons began to push me toward a return to Spain. I finally decided, in mid-1996, to leave the firm with which I had made my career and join a small firm in Madrid (founded two years earlier by two lawyers I knew well; one was the former New York foreign associate who had brokered my secondment several years before).

Almost simultaneously with this decision, my gambit with the Paris bar proved successful, and I proceeded with the paperwork to be admitted and was soon sworn in as an *avocat*. I only recently completed what I believe to be a unique "hat trick" of foreign admissions, and became admitted to practice as a Spanish *abogado*. This required convincing Spanish Ministry of Education officials that my common law degree was largely "homologable" (comparable) to the Spanish law degree, and passing a test in the courses in which they deemed my education to have been deficient, including such gems as Philosophy of Law, History of Spanish Law, and Roman Law, none of which I had studied as part of my J.D.

Since January 1997, then, I have been with the small Spanish firm, which has grown from four partners and one associate to five partners and eight associates, with steady future growth a sure prospect. My practice is not that dissimilar from my former practice in New York and Paris, although clearly less financial/banking in orientation and more corporate/commercial, and generally involving smaller, which does not necessarily mean easier, transactions. Indeed, all of my partners are former big-firm lawyers too. The philosophy of our firm has always been to try to handle transactions of similar size and scope to those handled by our respective former firms, but on a more personal basis, in a more congenial setting—and with (at least slightly) friendlier fees. To date, we are satisfied that we are achieving these goals and, as noted, have earned an enviable market niche.

D. WHAT ARE THE GOOD AND BAD THINGS ABOUT MY JOB?

There is a bit of a contradiction at the core of my current job, which accounts for some of its most positive aspects and some of its occasionally frustrating aspects.

I am an international lawyer in a very national setting; the great majority of our firm's work, and the majority of my work, is local in character. While I may have been practicing in Spain for several years and in Europe for a longer period and accumulating enough foreign admissions to line the wall behind my desk, I do not feel I am, and may never be, fully proficient and self-sufficient as a foreign lawyer. I will always need the assistance of locally trained and experienced colleagues. At the same time, I occasionally feel that my international skills are slipping, that if at one point I was on or near the "cutting edge" of international practice, such may no longer be the case. Instead, I sometimes think I am the stereotypical "jack of all trades and master of none."

But the chance to work on a broad variety of high-level matters in a small-firm setting is a great luxury in an age of ever-increasing specialization, sophistication, and competition in the legal marketplace. While perhaps I cannot realistically expect to be on the cutting edge of a particular aspect of financial law practice, as might be the case if I practiced in New York, London, or Paris with a major international firm, I have daily exposure to a diverse and satisfying range of work, quite likely more diverse and more satisfying than I would find in a large international firm.

E. WHAT ADVICE CAN I OFFER STUDENTS CONSIDERING INTERNATIONAL CAREERS IN LAW?

Certain things have surely changed since I set out on an international career. Globalization, the impact of the Internet, and all the related consequences have probably made it easier for one to commence an international career from any major U.S. city and with a far greater number of firms than may have been the case 15 or 20 years ago. Similarly, the number and variety of internationally active U.S. companies with legal departments that offer promising international career tracks have surely multiplied and will likely continue to increase, as U.S. companies, once their skills have been honed in the highly competitive domestic marketplace, look abroad for new markets in an increasingly uniform world. As a result, today's incipient international lawyer (or internationally active lawyer) probably has more varied points of entry available than his or her counterpart in the not-so-distant past.

In fact, U.S. lawyers have a clear competitive advantage in light of what has been referred to as the "Anglo-Saxonization" of global private practice. With English established as the international language of choice for the foreseeable future, the U.S./U.K. style of legal practice—based on proactive, commercially sensitive advice and involving detailed, carefully crafted contractual documentation—is making inroads into legal practice worldwide, even where civil code–based legal systems have historically used a much simpler approach to documentation.

At the same time, of course, the U.S. and U.K. firms, together with the giant accountancy firms and their legal affiliates, have established themselves as the most internationally aggressive players, and thus have opened more opportunities for beginning an international career.

For all of these reasons, today's law graduate may have a greater range of options available than did his or her predecessor ten or twenty years ago. But the skills and interests that such a lawyer brings to whatever post he or she finds remain unchanged and unchanging. These include, above all, an interest in understanding—and hopefully, in the interests of your clients, bridging to the extent possible—the obvious and not-so-obvious differences in approach, structure, and mind-set between U.S. law, lawyers, and their clients, on the one hand, and foreign law, foreign lawyers, and their clients and commercial and legal cultures, on the other. A New Yorker who cannot conceive of anything east of Long Island or south of Miami is not cut out for an international legal career. A lawyer who cannot learn, or feels incapable of learning, a foreign language or two is not cut out for an international career, nor is a lawyer who is convinced that the one and only way to solve a problem, draft an agreement, or structure a society is the American way.

A lawyer, on the other hand, who can explore other ways of dealing with a legal or commercial issue than the ways that work at home, and who can bring to bear the skills in another setting that the competitive U.S. market requires a lawyer to hone, should be well positioned for a satisfying and successful international legal career.

At the end of the day, questions of personal preferences and good luck are critical, and one may lead to the other. A young lawyer who opts for a career path that truly corresponds to his or her interests and abilities is likely to find an appropriate first professional opportunity, and a young lawyer who has found an appropriate first opportunity and works earnestly and diligently at developing legal practice skills is likely to find that the first opportunity will lead directly or indirectly to other opportunities, which may be even more interesting and more suited for the lawyer than any that he or she had envisioned.

In short, set your path carefully and work diligently, and good fortune should come your way.

Walking the High-Tech Wire: Going International with the Internet Generation

7

by Carolyn B. Herzog

A. INTRODUCTION

"For the last time, you cannot copy last week's 'Dilbert' cartoon into our software program."

"Why not?"

"Because it doesn't belong to our company and this use would constitute a copyright infringement. We don't own the rights."

Sometimes I think that my job is less lawyer and more parent or coach, gently trying to steer eager creative minds in the right direction and often being in a final "say so" position to determine whether that direction is in the best interests of the company. Occasionally, I need to determine the status of some pending legislation or the outcome of an important litigation related to my field of practice. But for the most part, I look to standard industry practice, headlines, experts in the field, treatises, online resources, and past practices, and then apply the all-encompassing "reasonable person" test. In today's changing legal market, the corporate legal department of a technology company offers lawyers valuable on-the-job experience for domestic and international legal issues, bringing classic legal training into some nontraditional spaces and cutting-edge legal conventions.

What does it mean to be an international "high-tech" lawyer today? It means that you can understand the letter of the law and can apply this specific knowledge reasonably and efficiently in a fast-paced business environment that often is on the cutting edge of technological developments and rapid global expansion. The next hot trend in dot-com land is not going to wait for you to write a ten-page memorandum on the pros and cons of a Ninth Circuit Court judge's opinion on the enforceability of shrink-wrap license agreements between U.S. and Japanese companies. You have one client—your company—and you need to have not only an understanding of your business, but the ability to explain the potential legal repercussions of taking one action over another. Weighing the risks against the benefits is a daily high-wire balancing act. When the deadline is upon you, your client *will* act and you have the distinct responsibility of counseling a multitude of talented and interesting people to ensure that the corporation's safety net is in place. From the vantage point of an in-house counsel to a U.S.-based multinational company, I will tell you about the type of practice that is available to you, how to get there, and what you can expect to encounter once you arrive.

B. TYPES OF PRACTICE: WHAT "IS" INTERNATIONAL?

There are international opportunities in almost every area of practice. The government is international—work for the U.S. Trade Representative, the Bureau of Export Affairs, the U.S. Agency for International Development, the Treasury Department, or even the Environmental Protection Agency and you will encounter issues that have a global impact. Law firms—small, medium, and large—are international and work on antitrust issues, litigation between U.S. and foreign companies, international transactions, and compliance of foreign companies with U.S. federal and state laws. Public interest lawyers are international—work for international organizations, trade associations, special-interest groups, or nonprofit organizations with international interests, such as human rights, environmental protection, software or music publishing, or international trade. Or, like me, you could work in-house for a multinational company, which could include manufacturers of food, energy, textiles, or technology.

But going global in the age of communication happens faster than ever and often doesn't allow lawyers the luxury of time to travel and meet to develop international strategies. As an in-house corporate lawyer, the opportunities to practice in an international environment are plentiful, but how this practice affects your lifestyle can vary greatly, depending on such varied elements as:

- Company size and volume of business
- The dimensions of your in-house legal department
- Special interests such as country-specific activities
- Customs and export needs
- Actions of regulatory agencies, treaties, trade conventions and other trends in the international community
- The expectations that have been set for your position
- Your particular interests and areas of expertise

Being an international lawyer doesn't require that you be the foremost expert on corporate tax entities in Saudi Arabia. However, if your company wants to do business in that country, you should know what questions to ask and where to find answers. Although your company may have offices worldwide and your breadth of work may encompass dealing with these international issues, you also won't necessarily travel extensively or become an expert in a specific area pertaining to international law. In-house lawyers tend to be more generalist in their practice so that they know what issues need to be addressed in a broad context and what questions need to be answered by experts in the field.

C. SKILL SETS FOR THE INTERNATIONAL LAWYER

Whereas the basic skill sets that you begin to learn about in law school and come to expect as a practitioner do not vary drastically, there are certainly differences in expectations, preparation, and application between other lawyers and in-house lawyers. We all draft language, write letters and documents, conduct research, enter into negotiations, and counsel our clients. But in-house lawyers will tend to be more involved in the business aspects of the corporate practice and often take into consideration the potential international aspects of every transaction, although it may initially be centered between U.S. companies. While providing advice on multiple levels and in multiple areas of law, in-house corporate lawyers often address considerations that can be more general in nature from a legal perspective and more specific from a business perspective. While a corporate lawyer in a law firm may be asked to provide specific advice about the particular meaning of a clause in a regulation, the in-house lawyer must take this information and apply it to the business concerns of the company on a domestic and an international level.

The following skill sets and preparatory tools are exemplary of those that should develop naturally as part of on-the-job training for any lawyer working in-house for a multinational company.

1. Spot the Issues

Regardless of the nature of your business, you must be aware of certain legal and business issues that have international implications. For instance, if you are shipping products overseas, setting up office, hiring employees, or providing services, you should be thinking of the following:

- **Delivery terms**—How is the product being shipped, electronically or via tangible property? The difference between FOB Destination or Origin may make a big difference in how your company can recognize the revenue from a purchase.

- **Payment terms**—Look for how many days it takes to pay, and the type and value of the currency in which your company might be paid or obligated to pay.

- **Tax implications**—Determine whether there is a treaty in place between the countries. Are there exemptions, could you be double-taxed, is there a route with lower taxes, or are there value-added tax implications?

- **Import/export regulations**—You may be responsible for filing for export licenses or working with foreign regulatory agencies to be able to import your products or services. Currently, the U.S. Department of Commerce, Bureau of Export Affairs has certain restrictions on the exportability of encryption products. Other countries, such as France and China, have varying laws on the importability of these same products.

- **Local corporate or tax regulations**—You may need to determine what type of office you should open—merely an operating office or a certain type of tax entity that may have local filing requirements.

- **Foreign regulatory permissions**—You may need to look at investment requirements, corporate filing requirements, technology licensing, general compliance, or registration of intellectual property rights (for example, for trademark law, is this a first-to-use or a first-to-file country; or, for copyrights, does this country recognize registrations for software code?).

- **Employment or labor law considerations**—Be aware that rights of employees and employer obligations may differ greatly from country to country. Employers need to be much more careful about hiring and firing employees in certain European countries where firing an employee, even for cause, could cost the employer up to six years of base pay.

- **Implied agency**—Where the United States may treat someone as an independent contractor, in some countries the very nature of an individual's job description could imply that he or she is actually an employee, thus triggering labor and tax issues again.

- **Political environment**—Find out if you are dealing with a public or private entity; foreign governments may have more regulatory control than we might assume in the United States, and in many countries privatization may take on various forms where seemingly private entities are actually branches of the government. Also, take into consideration ethical and political practices that may be prevalent in other countries where normal business practices may raise ethical conduct issues such as bribes, nepotism, privacy, dealing in black market goods, and other corrupt practices.

- **Enforceability of general contract terms**—Look for variations on standard indemnification, limits on liability, choice of law and venue, and what sorts of intellectual property protections are in place.

2. Learn the Business and Be Prepared

To effectively manage the legal considerations of running a business, a good in-house lawyer needs to coordinate with nearly every working group to ensure that each not only understands what function that group performs, but also that the members of that group know to consult their counsel when questions arise. You should anticipate spending significant time learning about the products and services, understanding the production process, educating yourself on marketing strategies, being informed on relevant accounting principles, participating in the innovation management process, and understanding the sales structure. An in-house counsel will likely work on the following tasks:

- Drafting and negotiating standard agreements such as technology licenses, confidentiality, distribution, consulting, professional services, leases, and employment agreements. These agreements may be both domestic and international in scope and, although dealing with the same products and services, may require different terms in different regions.

- Drafting and negotiating customized agreements such as development, OEM (original equipment manufacturer—where technologies are bundled and resold). These also may be based in one country and sold in others, or the bundle itself may involve more than one multinational company.

- Setting up joint ventures and strategic partnerships—these can vary from simple marketing and teaming agreements to more complicated corporate dealings.

- Corporate restructuring—through mergers and acquisitions, joint ventures, or for tax or other organizational purposes, your company's structure may be in a constant state of reorganization.

- Working with human resources on employment issues or benefits. An in-house lawyer may be involved in everything from establishing corporate policies on sexual harassment to drafting employment and severance agreements to implementation of stock option plans; benefits may vary from country to country, rights and obligations of the employer and employee may change, and issues pertaining to immigration often come into play.

- Developing and maintaining an innovation management program. Intellectual property is a hot area in law, and in-house lawyers should be responsible for registering, monitoring, and maintaining the trademark, patent, and copyright portfolios. This area includes working with marketing on branding, marketing materials, and press releases; working with engineering on keeping written records on innovations and filing for patent applications; and registering copyrights and marking products and materials with the appropriate proprietary markings.

- Read your Web site. This is part of a preventive practice. The information on your company's Web site could expose your company to issues such as copyright infringement, fraud, export issues, release of confidential information, and securities violations. Companies regularly use their Web site to describe the entire business and to conduct business. You need to be aware at all times what information is going on your Web site and where it is going.

- Litigation, mediation, and arbitration—Litigation management will run the gamut from labor relations and enforcement of agreements to protection of proprietary information and other corporate and securities-related matters. Many companies are choosing to include alternative methods of dispute resolution in their agreements as a first effort to resolve disputes.

- Training the company's employees on policies, procedures, and legal considerations and the company's clients on compliance with relevant U.S. and foreign laws.

- Selecting and managing outside counsel—choosing your own counsel wisely for tax, employment, securities, litigation, intellectual property protection and prosecution, and local law is no doubt one of the most important jobs an in-house lawyer must manage proficiently. You will need to monitor not only what this counsel is doing, but also the billing process, any implied agency issues, and the effectiveness of this counsel. You should trust your outside counsel implicitly and be aware when the counseling is not consistent with your own beliefs or needs. Your counsel should be business-savvy, understand your corporate culture, and practice preventive counseling to keep you out of trouble.

Expect differences between legal systems and learn to adapt. It can affect your perspective and help you to find solutions so that you are able to anticipate what is standard, expected, or fair before entering into negotiations.

3. Select Local Foreign Counsel

In selecting local foreign counsel, be aware of how the different societal and professional status of lawyers in other countries may affect your work. Pay attention to detail and do not assume similarities between legal systems. Women need to pay particular attention to issues that may affect gender. There will always be conflicts of interest, but you should position yourself to be as courteous and open to discussion as possible. Nevertheless, although flexibility is essential, make your position clear and decide how to best defend certain practices that are most important to you or handle those that are unacceptable in the United States. A thorough list of questions relating to the tasks at hand should help you reach your goal and select an effective counsel. Local counsel should be able to help you explain your position and should not be put in a position to defend or insist upon local laws or customs. Local counsel should be a trustworthy participant of your legal team and will ideally not only tell you what the law is, but also give you an advantage in negotiations and keep you out of trouble.

4. Consider the Culture

This is the time to walk in someone else's shoes. Pay attention to everything from dress style to negotiating style. For everyday social courtesies and in deciding what to wear, be conservative until you are certain of what is locally acceptable. Be attentive to body language and other means of communication, and pay close attention to the party you are addressing. Be as clear as possible and use examples or ask questions to be sure that both parties are understood. What may be considered forthright and "straight-shooting" in New York could very well kill a deal instantly in Brazil. A nod indicating yes may be interpreted as a no, and pondering on a maybe could be interpreted as a yes. Learn about the person you are dealing with, and make an effort to understand the behaviors and customs in a foreign environment. Always, even if you are proficient in the language, use a professional interpreter that you have selected and trust. Research the country in advance by reading books or talking with others who have traveled to or are from that area. Finally, pay attention to the time. You may need to get in earlier or stay later to accommodate the normal working hours in another country. Also, you should not expect that everyone works the hours of an American lawyer. Although an average workday may still involve the standard 12 to 14 hours, four of those may be spent at dinner, where conversations may be steered toward family and hobbies and not on the business at hand. It is not uncommon for people in other countries to judge your work ethic by your personality and family values, and not vice versa.

5. Use Reference Materials

Materials for in-house lawyers and international practitioners often are vastly different from those that a trusts and estates lawyer would use in Wisconsin. Due to groundbreaking developments and the resulting changing business practices, the in-house international practitioner must be creative, looking to unconventional resources and comparing practices in more than one region. Rather than looking to the U.S. Code or the *Federal Register*, you would more likely refer to treatises, such as Michael Epstein and Frank Politano's "Drafting License Agreements" or Richard Kirkpatrick's "Likelihood of Confusion in Trademark Law," and guides such as *The ABA Guide to International Business Negotiations, 2nd edition.* The Internet currently has a wealth of international resources that can lead you to drafts of regulations currently being debated, foreign government resources, and information published by international organizations such as the United Nations, the International Bank for Reconstruction and Development (IBRD), the World Intellectual Property Organization (WIPO), and agencies within the European Union. And well-known legal resources, such as LEXIS-NEXIS and WestLaw, often have service packages that are directed toward international issues.

D. HOW TO PREPARE

You can prepare for a career in international law through education, work experience and internships, memberships in professional organizations, networking activities, and international travel. Developing a career that takes you to other countries and introduces you to foreign ideas, customs, practices, and knowledge is not a difficult task, but it takes more than a click of the mouse to gain international experience.

1. Explore Opportunities

A possible first introduction to international law is the choice that we all make in the various stages of our education. Whether it's studying a foreign language at the undergraduate level or taking a comparative international law course during law school, there are multiple opportunities for exposure to an international environment in school. For me, choosing to go to law school was the second tier of my career choice. The first tier was international. I looked for schools that had strong programs in international law, but that was not the only factor I considered when evaluating law schools and opportunities with international exposure. Although the school that I ultimately chose, the University of Wisconsin–Madison, was not as highly regarded for its international focus as some of the more obvious choices in Washington, D.C., where I was living at the time, the *International Law Journal* was respected, the International Law Students' Association was active, I completed many courses in international and comparative law with esteemed professors, and the in-state tuition allowed me to take advantage of opportunities overseas that I might not otherwise have been able to afford. The criteria that I looked for included job opportunities or other work experience, prospects for travel, visiting lectures, the international experience of the professors, and the overall flexibility in the academic program.

The array of interesting internships, clerkships, part-time jobs, and clinical programs available to law students today is vast. Many schools administer legal training programs locally and internationally for which students can apply and even prepare for well in advance. Some schools have clinical programs that allow students to experience the practical application of their studies—through drafting, preparing documents for court appearances, listening to clients and observing lawyers' responses, and even legislative tracking. Look for visiting lecturers from other countries or useful standard courses such as an introduction to international business transactions or comparative law. Don't limit yourself to your school if it doesn't offer the kind of opportunity that you are looking for. Explore opportunities at other universities, in the United States and in countries that interest you. Be prepared, however, to do considerable research on the legal system and methods of teaching and practicing. At the very least, you should be prepared to learn the major differences between a civil-law system and a common-law system. And, keep an open mind and consider cultural and historical differences when applying your personal perceptions to foreign law.

Even before we begin our legal studies in the United States, the majority of us have preconceived notions about the status of a law that we most likely picked up from popular media. There is a common phenomenon that occurs among first-year law students that annoys all of our nonlawyer acquaintances to the point of exclusion. We cannot resist watching television shows about cops and lawyers and declaring to anyone who cares to listen that the actor playing the police officer, lawyer or judge is dead wrong in their assessment. We also love to scream "hearsay" and other rules of evidence during trial procedures. We know it's obnoxious, but we can't help showing off our newfound knowledge to prove that we actually do know a tidbit or two about criminal law. This same principle applies to the practice of international law. Once we learn a little about domestic law, we have to be extremely careful to avoid drawing conclusions that the American way of thinking is the exclusive avenue to finding a legal solution.

2. Be Enterprising

I learned many lessons about wrong assumptions while studying and working in France. As a devout Francophile, I wanted to spend a period during law school in France or in a French-speaking country. I found a summer job in a French law firm in Paris by applying through the Tulane law school program because the University of Wisconsin only had exchange programs in Germany, Chile, and the Netherlands. I worked while attending classes at Tulane's summer program that focused on European Union law. I then arranged an individual exchange with the University of Paris with the assistance of a law school professor who managed an exchange program in Germany and a French law school professor whom I had met at the Tulane summer program. The exchange, while challenging to orchestrate and complete (oral exams in French and different methods of lecturing and learning were required), was one of the most rewarding experiences of my career.

One way to find opportunities and meet people who have explored nontraditional international experiences is to maintain memberships in professional organizations relating to your field of interest. When I returned to Washington, D.C., after finishing law school, I immediately called the Section of International Law and Practice of the ABA. I was amazed at the resources I could access as a student, and I am continually appreciative of the personal and practical resources that are available to me as a professional. I looked for committees to join that had topics that interested me, such as protection of copyright on the Internet and the international e-commerce committee, and for places where I could find mentorship, which is how I eventually came to co-chair the Section's Women's Interest Network.

Through this network, I have met women who have excelled in their fields and are willing to share their experiences in international law and learning from others. I also have met many men who share similar interests and are interested in expanding their networks. In fact, I met my future employer while organizing a networking event relating to a new development in technology because of my personal interest in the topic.

Another way to expand your network is to participate in local bar events and local councils, such as the High Technology Council of Maryland and the Northern Virginia Technology Council. Look for other local, national, and international associations with common interests, such as the American Corporate Counsel Association, the Association of Women in International Trade (WIIT), the Union Internationale des Avocats, and Women in Technology International (WITI). Either through informational interviews or through substantive meetings and networking events, speaking with lawyers in law firms that represent technology companies or venture capitalists that invest in technology companies (or any other type of company that interests you) can be a great way to learn about opportunities. Never underestimate the power of a handshake and a smile. Your next employer could likely be a contact from a presentation on a topic of mutual interest, networking event, professional association meeting, or even through social events in your area like art shows or benefits.

E. WHERE ARE THE JOBS AND HOW CAN YOU FIND THEM?

Beginning the dreaded job hunt is a daunting task. Finding the right job is a skill set in and of itself. It requires some self-awareness, perseverance, the ability to set goals and create plans to achieve those goals, and education about the job market. When I graduated from law school, there was one international job resource in our career center—a four-year-old application for the Foreign Service. On-campus interviews were generally linked to midwestern law firms and followed a random-number system that ran secondary to a top 10 percent ranking. After working for the World Bank for four years prior to law school, I was severely disappointed to realize that my fellow classmates and I were being herded into interviews where personal interests and strengths were virtually irrelevant. Although many schools have state-of-the art career centers with vast libraries and contacts, it's important to learn about the various resources that are available to job hunters today.

1. First Stop—the Internet

There are numerous job-posting and career-assistance Web sites available today at little or no cost to the job hunter. Some sites allow you to post your résumé and receive access to mail rooms where interested employers will provide you notices of positions. Still others, such as emplawyernet.com, allow you to fill out a form indicating your interests, from areas of practice to geographic locations, and will then send you notices of positions that meet your criteria. The Internet also is a great tool to look for information on companies, press announcements, and even hiring trends and salary expectations. Many employers in both the public sector and the technology sector now have job announcements on their Web sites and instructions for applying online.

Headhunter and recruiter contacts are generally more useful once you've obtained some experience. Some are friendlier than others and may be more willing to assist new graduates or people considering new fields. When I first returned to Washington, D.C., prepared to begin my job search, I contacted a well-known recruiter who also was the aunt of a friend. I thought I had an "in." She essentially told me that I would never find the job I was looking for and that I should return to Wisconsin. Not two years later, this same recruiter called me looking for contacts, forgetting that we had spoken before. Helping others brings its rewards. Whether it is providing referrals, volunteering to help on a committee, or just being open to speak about your interests, making the right contacts is rewarding on many levels.

The contacts that you meet through networking activities, lawyers in firms, meetings of special interest, and even social events are highly valuable, but this shouldn't negate doing your own research. And, although the Internet is a magnificent tool, you should read pertinent newspapers, magazines, and trade journals.

F. ACHIEVING BALANCE

1. The Upside, the Downside, and Everything In Between

Working in the legal department of a mid-size publicly traded corporation has afforded me the kind of lifestyle, practice, and experience that, I believe, are best suited for my current goals. The benefits are good; the hours are sometimes long but fairly flexible and rarely include weekends; the

practice area is at the same time trendy and traditional; and the opportunities for advancement can arrive almost too quickly.

The pay in-house is generally not as high as in a large law firm, but it
is generally comparable to mid-size firm salaries; greater than most areas
of academia, government, and public interest sectors; and often offers an
additional benefit of stock options and an end-of-year bonus. The increased
competition in the technology sector has caused firms in areas with a high
concentration of technology companies to increase their salaries to attract
the best and the brightest. They also provide benefit packages that include
two to three weeks of vacation, 401(k) plans, competitive healthcare packages, and other incentives, such as participation in cafeteria plans, assistance with child care, or contributions to health club memberships. There
is, in general, a greater focus on family and on employee relations than is
attributed to a large law firm style of practice.

Working in-house does grant you more free time than the average starting associate. However, don't expect to work an eight-hour day and go
home free of work obligations. You are far less likely to be handed a client
project on Friday at 6 p.m. that has to be completed by Monday at 9 a.m.,
but remember that you have one client that you clearly can't afford to lose
and the doctor is always on call. Because your job is sometimes confused,
resented, or conveniently forgotten until trouble strikes, you will need to
practice as much preventive medicine as possible to prepare for foreseeable trouble spots. In addition, time management and allocation of tasks
can be very different in an in-house environment. You may have larger
long-term projects that pertain to the method of your practice or overall
compliance, and yet have to deal with everyday issues such as corporate
matters from executive management, sales that have to close that day from
sales associates, and the urgent press release from the marketing department. You will likely need to reset your priorities many times in one day.

You will get more hands-on experience by preparing for trouble spots
and handling the unexpected on a fast-paced, day-to-day basis. You are not
likely to become the nation's foremost expert on Article 2B of the Uniform
Commercial Code, but you will learn, generally, how it affects your business. This experience will vary again depending on the size of the company and its in-house legal department. Very large companies, such as the
large telecommunications firms, may have as many lawyers as a mid-size
firm, and this in-house department will likely operate in a similar fashion

to a law firm—practice areas are more segregated, and crossover between practice areas can be extremely limited. Large companies also may have different reporting structures. In a smaller corporation, most lawyers report directly to the general counsel. In a larger corporation, lawyers may be organized by region or practice areas and report to separate general counsels or heads of business units. Although larger companies may limit your access to a broader range of legal issues, they can offer you superior opportunities for hands-on experience and greater expertise in a more specific practice area.

The opportunities for advancement in the in-house environment are very different from the more structured environments in law firms or the government sector. An in-house counsel doesn't have a level based on years with the firm, or a grade number based on a regulated organization. In the rapidly expanding technology industry, opportunities for advancement are offered to those with particular expertise in the field. As a third- or fourth-year lawyer, you may find yourself managing a legal department in a smaller corporation or a division of a legal department in a larger corporation. Technology companies appreciate enthusiasm, willingness to cooperate, loyalty, creative thinking, and a good sense of business.

If you are looking for international travel experience, working in-house may not be your best bet unless you are placed in a foreign office. In such a position, you are more likely to hire outside counsel to do the traveling for you or local counsel. Your personal geographic or cultural preferences also will play a big part in where and how you choose to practice law. If you have an affinity for the West Coast lifestyle, you may want to choose a field in entertainment law in Los Angeles, technology in Silicon Valley, or Pacific Rim–related business. If you prefer New York, you may end up in the financial district or on Wall Street. If your preference is regulatory or technological, look to the metropolitan D.C. area for Internet, telecommunications-related, and biotechnology-related businesses. If you have a strong interest in some foreign culture and possess some language capabilities and the desire to live overseas, you may want to investigate larger companies that are more likely to have legal staff in countries where they conduct a significant amount of business. Whereas in my medium-size company I manage our overseas offices in Europe, Asia, Africa, and South America from our corporate headquarters, a larger company may choose to have in-house staff in multiple geographic areas.

G. CONCLUSION

Whether you ultimately choose private practice, government work, academia, or corporate in-house practice, the choice is ultimately a personal one, based on environment, lifestyle, areas of interest, and long-term goals. Your background may influence your decisions, including undergraduate and graduate education, work experience, travel, language capabilities, and other special talents. Being an effective counsel is more about spotting issues, understanding the business, and applying knowledge in a practical and reasonable manner than it is about memorizing case law or writing brilliant legal briefs or memoranda on specific areas of law. Research on other cultures and business practices is vital preparation, but international exposure through work or travel is important in order to be able to learn and understand different legal systems and cultures. Do your research, study the company, meet your potential colleagues, and determine whether the overall environment suits your goals and personality. Working in-house for a technology company can be an extremely rewarding experience if the pieces fit—it's fast-paced, cutting-edge, multinational, and touches upon the major issues that any international lawyer would encounter in a business environment. Although I could not recommend relying on stock options as the primary incentive for accepting any job, who knows—if the stock price is right and the market favors your company, *you too could be a millionaire!*

Changes in Direction in a Legal Career

8

by Nancy D. Israel

A. INTRODUCTION

This chapter illustrates the different directions a legal career can take over time. In my 20 years in practice, I have been an international lawyer, a litigator, and a business lawyer. I have practiced in both big and small law firms and as in-house counsel in the private sector, for a multinational professional services firm, and in the nonprofit sector, for a university. When I wrote a chapter for the first edition of this book, I was international counsel to one of the big accounting firms; I currently practice in a small law firm in suburban Boston.

My firm, Erickson Schaffer Peterson Israel & Silberman, provides legal advice on international and domestic business matters. I counsel clients on business issues from start-up through expansion and exit, including establishment, foreign expansion, intellectual property protection, employment matters, and mergers and acquisitions. I concentrate on general counsel services, foreign business arrangements, assessments of insurers' liability risks, computer systems integration contracts, and sophisticated commercial negotiations. My clients range from emerging companies to multinational institutions. I also represent individuals on occasion. Given my background, a substantial portion of my clients are in the service industry, such as Web-based services, insurance, and financial services firms.

My level of involvement with a client varies with the client's needs. For some small and mid-size clients I serve as outside general counsel, a role I much enjoy; it allows me to work closely with businesspeople and to provide general advice and counsel. For other clients, particularly large institutions, I may become deeply involved in a particular area and provide ongoing advice and services related to that area. For still others, I am involved only on a transactional basis.

After 20 years of practicing law in different fields and settings, I find myself with an enjoyable and challenging practice in an environment that allows me some reasonable balance between my professional and personal lives. Given the serendipitous way in which my career has developed, I know that for some of us there is no clearly defined road map to our careers.

B. THE KNOCK OF OPPORTUNITY

Although I had wanted to be a lawyer since I was 12 and an international lawyer since I studied Russian in high school, I had not, I thought, followed a course that would lead to international law. The opportunity came out of the blue. After Harvard College and Harvard Law School (and five months of backpacking around the world), I became a litigation associate for the Boston law firm of Hale & Dorr. I chose Hale & Dorr after I called someone I knew there to advise me on which New York law firm I should join and he suggested joining Hale & Dorr instead. My practice was about half civil (trade secrets, environmental, contracts, and general business litigation) and half criminal (Medicare fraud, bank robbery, etc.). I had some trial experience, a lot of motion practice, and a lot of client contact.

Three and one-half years later, as a consequence of a chance remark at a cocktail party, I applied to and then joined the Office of the General Counsel at Harvard University. While at Harvard I had a general practice, concentrating in litigation, environmental law, athletics, corporate governance, and government and community affairs. I worked on such matters as designing and implementing a compliance program for what was then a new state hazardous-waste labeling law, a bid protest on a government contract, sex discrimination lawsuits, and a nuclear-free-zone referendum. Because the office was just developing, I also became involved in law office management issues, such as whether we should keep timesheets (we did not), whether we should specialize (we did not), and even choosing the artwork from the university's collection (unfortunately, we decided on a large Audubon print of a wild turkey for the entryway, leading to predictable comments about lawyers).

After about two years, on a snowy evening, I attended a bar association dinner at the invitation of the general counsel of what was then Arthur Young & Company (one of what, at the time, were the "Big 8" accounting firms). During dinner he offered me the opportunity to do international work. After much deliberation, and extracting a promise that I would not have to crunch numbers (I am not a C.P.A., and one of the attractions of law school had been that it seemed to promise a career relatively free of numbers), I accepted the offer.

C. SINK OR SWIM

My first day on the job I was handed some articles of association for a Cayman Islands mutual company. I barely knew where the Cayman Islands were and did not know what a mutual company was. I also found that my major clients were all well over six feet tall, male, and dubious.

From that inauspicious beginning I continued for close to ten years as the international counsel of Arthur Young and then of its successor firm, Ernst & Young. I was fortunate to be a partner during the years when the Big 8 firms were transforming themselves from accounting firms to professional services firms, from affiliations of domestic partnerships in various countries to multinational organizations, and from the "Big 8" to the "Big 6" (and now the "Big 5"). I also was fortunate to be in a role in which I had significant contact with senior people in the other Big 8 firms. Consequently, I had invaluable experience in business transformations, as well as in international legal matters. I also was exposed to strategic thinking and a service ethos at Ernst & Young and the other Big 8 firms that I have tried to incorporate into my own practice.

After I left Ernst & Young to return to Boston, I became of counsel to the Boston law firm of Hill & Barlow and chair of the international law practice group. During my three years at Hill & Barlow I worked primarily on developing the international law practice, as well as on general corporate and business law matters.

I decided to join what is now known as Erickson Schaffer Peterson Israel & Silberman, a small firm that was relatively new, because of its focus on international (as well as domestic) business law and because most of the lawyers had come from big law firms and/or had served as in-house

counsel to big companies. More generally, I had decided that I was sufficiently interested in business to want to have my own business, although
not so interested in business that I wanted to leave the practice of law.
Finally, I hoped (and since have found) that I would be able to control my
practice to the extent that is possible in the law and, accordingly, would be
able to combine a quality practice with family life.

D. THE IMPORTANCE OF BACKGROUND

I think a varied general and legal background has served me well and would
be good preparation for anyone wishing to enter the field of international
law. Similarly, I think my liberal arts education was solid preparation for
law school. My undergraduate degree is in social studies, an interdiscipli-
nary major in history, government, philosophy, and political science. I took
many courses in international relations. Although I took some international
law courses in law school, as with all lawyers my real training came through
the actual practice of law. The summer after my first year of law school and
thereafter during the year, I researched antitrust issues for the New York
law firm of Weil, Gotshal & Manges. During the summer after my second
year I worked on natural resources issues (my then-interest) and property
matters for a mid-size Los Angeles law firm (called Nossaman, Krueger &
Marsh at the time).

My experiences as international counsel of Ernst & Young are particularly interesting. Ernst & Young is one of the largest professional services
organizations in the world. I served as the international legal counsel to the
U.S. firm, to the worldwide organization, and to member firms and associated entities in other countries as needed. My "client" at Ernst & Young
consisted of numerous legal entities providing a wide variety of services in
over 100 countries. My clientele was primarily senior management in the
various entities I represented. Many of the services I provided related to
the interfirm relations within the Ernst & Young organization, although I
also gave advice to the firm related to licensing and contractual arrangements with its clients and other third parties. As an in-house lawyer, I did
not provide legal services to clients of the firm.

E. LARGE-FIRM ADVANTAGES

While at Ernst & Young I particularly enjoyed my role as a general adviser
and counselor on international business matters. In addition to legal advice

I provided input on business and policy issues. Because I was close to the businesspeople and was intimately familiar with the policies and practices of the firm, I was included in the structuring of transactions and the decision making at an early stage. A substantial amount of my practice concerned intellectual property protection of proprietary methodologies and software. Another significant area of my practice was structuring worldwide distribution arrangements. Typically I worked with local counsel in figuring out what protections were available, enforceable, and feasible in a particular country. Generally the issues ranged from licensing, trademark, and contractual issues to export-import issues, to tax issues, to foreign exchange and financing issues. On one project, I worked with local counsel in 30 countries to develop adequate legal and practical protections for the software distributed in those countries.

Another component of my practice was establishing, revising, and dissolving business structures. For example, I drafted a joint-venture agreement and related incorporation documents for a Korean joint venture, established various forms of limited-liability companies in offshore locations, and helped the member firms in such varied locales as Trinidad, Nigeria, Turkey, and Indonesia revise their partnership agreements. One of the more complex organizational matters I worked on evolved out of the merger of Arthur Young and Ernst & Whinney, the combination that produced Ernst & Young. I recommended and then established the legal structure of the new international organization. This task involved researching forms of business entities in jurisdictions such as Switzerland, the Netherlands, Guernsey, and Bermuda; meeting with the leadership of the international organization to propose the structure and jurisdiction I recommended; drafting the organizational documents; finding local service providers; and terminating the international organizations of the predecessor firms.

At Ernst & Young I negotiated and drafted all types of what one of my clients called "whereas, what for, why not, love and kisses" service agreements. For example, I reviewed contracts for financial consulting services to be provided in Hungary and Iraq. I drafted documents for an executive search business in Korea. Negotiating and drafting those types of agreements remains part of my practice. I have negotiated a service agreement for a credit card service provider to provide certain services in Canada, a Web site design/build consulting agreement for an emerging company that provides e-commerce solutions, and contracts for state entities to purchase multimillion-dollar integrated computer systems.

F. OPERATING ACROSS BORDERS

While the particular skills I developed at Ernst & Young concerning organizational structures in various countries, intellectual property protection, and complex commercial negotiations have proven quite useful, my general familiarity with operating across borders and in different legal systems has been of even greater use. Moreover, I can call upon the network of contacts I established with law firms around the world, and within the Big 5 firms, to serve my clients wherever they may be doing business.

A final area to which I devoted substantial time at Ernst & Young is risk management. Among other things, I was involved in structuring Ernst & Young's professional indemnity insurance arrangements. In that capacity, I monitored litigation outside of the United States and provided assistance in analyzing the risk posed by such litigation. That aspect of my practice involved meeting with foreign counsel to review local laws, procedures, and litigation strategy. I became familiar with different types of insurance arrangements, such as the Lloyd's market and mutual and captive insurance vehicles, as well as with dealing with insurers in financial difficulty. The intellectual challenge made insurance and risk assessment one of the more interesting areas of my practice.

G. SMALL-FIRM ADVANTAGES

In my present practice I devote a considerable amount of time to representation of major insurers and reinsurers. I advise them on their liability risks arising from certain professional indemnity insurance programs they cover. Using the knowledge I have developed over many years, I assist them in analyzing their potential exposure from claims around the world covered by those programs. I also provide related advice on such matters as coverage issues, drafting reinsurance policies, and identifying worldwide trends in liability risks. One of the benefits of practicing law in a small firm is that I have been able to act as outside general counsel to some of my small and mid-sized clients, a role that I found more difficult to develop in the economics of a big law firm environment. As an outside lawyer, however, I have not become as involved in the business decisions as I was as in-house counsel.

H. OTHER FORUMS

Not all of my experience has come from practicing law. For many years I was very active in bar association activities. I served several terms in the House of Delegates of the ABA and on the Board of Delegates of the Massachusetts Bar Association. I was on the Council of the ABA's Section of International Law and Practice. These and other bar association and law-related activities introduced me to people from all over the country and all types of law practices. Participating in such activities as heading a section, allocating grant money, serving on editorial boards, and pro bono work has helped my negotiating and managerial skills, as have my experiences in serving on boards of directors of nonprofit organizations, such as the International Institute of Boston and the Harvard Alumni Association.

Continuing legal education is another way not only to hone skills, but also to make contacts in the field. I have organized, presented, and attended numerous educational programs, some of which have provided lasting contacts. For example, some years ago I attended the American Center for International Leadership Europe–America Emerging Leaders Conference, where I met lawyers from Eastern and Western Europe and Mexico. I also met a lawyer from Massachusetts who became one of my partners.

Each opportunity has led to other opportunities, and my career has developed in ways I could not have predicted. I feel fortunate to be a member of a profession in which it is possible to have such a varied career and to have had such a diverse exposure to the law. If I have any career advice for others, it is simply to not be afraid to change direction and to fashion a practice that suits your own personality and interests.

The Practice of International Trade Law in the Public Sector

9

by Eleanor Roberts Lewis[1]

A. INTRODUCTION

Someday as a young lawyer you will have a difficult choice to make. Should you work for a private law firm where you will represent specific paying clients, where the hours are almost always long but the financial rewards are generally very high? Or should you enter public service, where you will earn a more modest income but have the opportunity to serve over 275 million American citizens and enjoy a more balanced lifestyle?

After earning my J.D. at Georgetown University, I went to work as a staff lawyer for the U.S. Department of Housing and Urban Development (HUD). I initially chose the public sector because of my interest in the public policy aspects of law and because I hoped the federal government would provide a supportive environment for a mother with a newborn child. After two years at HUD I received a good

1.   I would like to thank Allyson L. Senie, a senior counsel at the U.S. Department of Commerce, for her substantial assistance in the preparation of this chapter, particularly the section on lifestyle issues. I also would like to thank paralegal Pamela Jessen for her work on the summaries of international legal opportunities in federal agencies. Of course, the views expressed in this chapter are my own and not those of any other person or U.S. government agency.

offer from a private law firm and decided to try it out. I learned many important things during my three years in private practice, including the discipline to focus on the needs of a particular client. But I missed being on the front lines of public policy issues. And I did not find law firms at that time to be very family-friendly. So I returned to HUD, this time as head lawyer for the Government National Mortgage Association and the public housing finance program.

In 1982 I was offered the opportunity to set up a new legal office at the U.S. Department of Commerce to focus on the market access and transactional aspects of international trade and investment. Until then, the existing international legal offices at Commerce concentrated primarily on the regulatory aspects of trade, such as export controls and anti-dumping/ countervailing duties. I hesitated to accept the position, having practiced only project finance and other areas of real estate law for eight years. I had studied international law academically but had never practiced in the field outside the finance context. "A woman's response," said my mentor at the time. He noted that women often assume they must be expert in a field before applying for or accepting a job, while men generally assume they can learn on the job. Suggesting that any good lawyer could master any subject in a few months or even a few weeks, he advised that I buy some books on trade law and accept the position. I followed his advice, although it took more than a few months and a few books for me to become truly comfortable with such a major change in professional specialties.

It proved to be a worthwhile move. Since I began work at the Commerce Department, I have dealt almost daily with both interesting and important matters. Some of the legal problems and work environment issues in the public practice of trade law are similar to those found in private practice, but many are different in ways that may make a public-sector career particularly appealing. This chapter will discuss specific examples of the substantive work, as well as personal considerations, involved in being an international trade lawyer in the public sector, concluding with a brief description of some federal agencies that employ international trade lawyers.

B. WHY PRACTICE WHAT THEY TEACH?

Many of us now practicing international law took at least one course in college or law school on general international law, trade law, or comparative law. As a student I realized that these subjects entailed an especially complex and even exotic mixture of legal and policy issues that were domestic, foreign, and multinational in scope. The practice of trade law in the public sector more than lives up to the intellectual expectations engendered by the academic environment. It also offers possibilities for travel and exposure to diverse cultures that I had not explored in school. Consider these illustrative examples from my own career.

1. Trade Agreements

My most high-profile and exciting work involves being part of interagency teams that negotiate, interpret, and enforce trade and investment agreements with foreign governments. During the course of my career in trade law, I have worked on diverse, challenging assignments related to negotiation and implementation of the U.S.-Canada Free Trade Agreement and its successor, the North American Free Trade Agreement (NAFTA); the World Trade Organization (WTO) agreements; the U.S.-Japan Automotive Agreement; the OECD Convention on Bribery; and bilateral investment treaties with such diverse countries as Poland, Tunisia, and Argentina.

The goal of NAFTA was the substantial elimination of trade and investment barriers between the United States, Canada, and Mexico in order to create a market with almost 400 million consumers, almost $7 trillion in annual output, and over $500 billion in annual trade. With approximately 1,000 pages of legal text and 1,000 pages of tariff schedules, much was riding on every NAFTA word and number. In addition to fairly common provisions on tariff and customs matters, NAFTA for the first time covered in detail nontariff issues such as trade in services, intellectual property rights, and investment, as well as sanitary/phytosanitary measures (agricultural standards). Government lawyers played an important role in shaping NAFTA, which in turn strongly influenced the WTO negotiations under way at the same time. My work on NAFTA was not limited to technical legal issues; it entailed contributions to policy development and representation of diverse U.S. agency and private-sector interests.

The relatively new OECD Convention on Bribery also will have an important impact on U.S. commercial interests. It has been estimated that U.S. firms have been losing many billions of dollars a year because their foreign competitors pay bribes to win foreign government business. Since 1977 U.S. firms have been prohibited from making such payments by the Foreign Corrupt Practices Act (FCPA). This convention, the product of almost eight years of discussion and negotiations, internationalizes the basic principle of the FCPA: no person may offer, promise, or give any money or other advantage to a foreign public official to obtain or retain business. In this convention, for which my office provided critical drafting and negotiating support, the governments of other developed countries agree to adopt the same high, anticorruption standard to which U.S. law holds U.S. companies in their international transactions.

2. Trade-related Legislation, Dispute Settlement, and Litigation

The negotiation of NAFTA, WTO, and numerous other trade and investment agreements requires extensive involvement by government lawyers. In addition, government lawyers play an essential role in the development and drafting of related legislation. For example, the bill drafted by the Executive Branch to implement NAFTA was about 450 pages long and was accompanied by a 260-page "statement of administrative action" to explain the provisions of the agreement and legislation. Although lawyers from the U.S. Trade Representative's Office take the lead in drafting such legislative documents (as they generally do in trade negotiations), lawyers from my office and several other agencies are an essential part of the inter-agency team that produces the final product.

After trade agreements become effective, government lawyers continue to play an important role in assessing whether our foreign trading partners are complying with their obligations. When it seems they do not, we assist in consultations with the foreign governments to encourage compliance. If our consultations are unsuccessful, we advise on the application of domestic trade laws as well as assist the U.S. Trade Representative with the dispute settlement cases that may be brought under NAFTA and WTO.

Trade agreements are sometimes challenged in court, such as the currently pending case on the constitutionality of NAFTA.[2] Interesting issues also arise about the allocation of appropriate government roles in the commercial and foreign policy arenas. For example, in one of our cases the Supreme Court decided that the state of Massachusetts did not have the right to institute unilateral economic sanctions against Burma when the U.S. federal government had already developed an elaborate framework to address human rights abuses by that country.[3] Although the Justice Depart-

---

2.   Made in the USA Foundation v. U.S., 56 F. Supp. 2d 1226 (N.D. Ala. 1999).

3.   Crosby v. National Foreign Trade Council, 120 S. Ct. 2288 (2000).

ment is responsible for filing the briefs and making the oral arguments in such cases, lawyers from Commerce and other affected U.S. agencies are extensively involved in the process.

3. Advice and Advocacy for U.S. Exporters and Investors

The daily "bread and butter" of some lawyers in my office is counseling U.S. firms and their lawyers about questions or problems that arise in foreign business transactions. Issues range from formation of contracts and hiring of agents/distributors to protection of intellectual property rights and settlement of commercial disputes. The U.S. government also has an aggressive program to support U.S. firms bidding for foreign government contracts. The international government procurement market amounts to hundreds of billions of dollars a year. Many interesting and often complex legal and policy issues arise with respect to which companies and products the U.S. government should support and how that support should be offered.

4. Technical Assistance for Foreign Countries

An exciting and gratifying role for lawyers at Commerce is to provide technical legal assistance to foreign governments trying to establish a market economy and seeking advice on how to develop the necessary underlying commercial legal structure. Generally, these countries are converting from a communist or other centralized economic system. But sometimes they are recovering from domestic turmoil. Examples of countries we have assisted include Russia, China, South Africa, and most of the countries of Eastern Europe.

5. Equal and Better Opportunities

The practice of international trade law with the U.S. government virtually guarantees inherently interesting and important assignments. It also offers other advantages. Because government offices almost always have more work than they can handle, young lawyers typically are given more responsibility earlier than they ordinarily would have it in a law firm. A government lawyer right out of law school can expect in the first year to have direct client contact and a relatively independent caseload, as well as opportunities to represent his or her office in interagency meetings. Within two years of employment, most lawyers in my office have participated in negotiations with foreign government officials.

In addition, the federal government takes seriously the legal require-ment and public policy goal that women, minorities, and other disadvan-taged persons be given an equal opportunity to succeed. For example, although women have constituted over 40 percent of law school classes for many years, only 15 percent of the partners in private law firms are women. By contrast, 25 percent of all government GS-15–level lawyers (equivalent in experience and stature to partners) are women. And almost as high a percentage of government Senior Executive Service (SES) lawyers are women. (SES legal positions are similar to senior or managing partners in law firms.) The statistics for minority lawyers similarly reflect the more welcoming and upwardly mobile environment of the public sector.

C. BALANCING FAMILY AND WORK: THE LIFESTYLE ISSUE

What does all this talk about balancing family and work mean in real life? Start with the morning. Instead of just getting yourself up, dressed, fed, and out the door for your daily commute, it may be you plus one or two or more. You may be caring for young children, an elderly live-in parent, or a sick family member who must be prepared for their daily routine as well. This usually entails getting them up, dressed, and fed before turning them over to a daytime caregiver. Whatever the scenario, you must build an extra hour or more into morning activities before turning your attention to work once you finally reach your desk. Now fast-forward through your day and picture the evening ritual of racing to leave the office to pick up your de-pendents from the day care provider. Your colleagues have one more ques-tion, your boss needs one more item researched; you download the memo you have been working on onto a floppy disk, promising yourself you will return to it once the rest of the family is in bed. You answer the phone one last time and fly out of the office, late again.

Congress and the Executive Branch have become increasingly sensi-tized to the inherent stresses of balancing work and family. A major driv-ing force behind this sensitization is the increasing number of women who choose to or must work outside the home while continuing to shoulder major family responsibilities. By 1998, more than 40 percent of women caring for children under three years old were working outside the home, and almost 80 percent of women with children from six to 17 were in the labor force.

Another driving force is the realization by men that spending time ac-tively assisting in the day-to-day activities of child rearing or caring for elderly or sick family members is important and may even be a necessity when both parents work. All of the male lawyers in my office have excellent credentials and most have had jobs with first-rate private law firms. However, these bright, dedicated men, as well as the exceptional women lawyers in my office, have chosen public service not only for its interesting, important work, but also for the more balanced lifestyle it provides compared to private practice.

A balanced lifestyle does not always mean shorter hours. When a major project entails demanding deadlines, a government lawyer can work as long and travel as much as any private-sector lawyer. However, in a government legal office there will rarely be the pressure to work late into the night or show up on the weekends just to compete and impress. Fortunately, the federal government has implemented a number of programs to help employees balance family and professional responsibilities.

1. Flexible Work Schedules

In 1994, the President issued a memorandum to executive agencies directing them to establish programs to support flexible, family-friendly work arrangements. Since then, federal employees have been able to choose part-time employment, job-sharing arrangements, telecommuting, and alternative work schedules permitting flexible hours and compressed workdays. Government studies show that these flexible workplace programs improve recruitment, lower absenteeism, and increase morale and retention of good employees.

2. Child Care

As of 1999, over 110 federal child-care centers were operating in or near federal buildings in over 30 states and the District of Columbia. The hours of operation at these centers vary, but almost 90 percent are open 11 or more hours per day. Over 90 percent also offer infant care, generally beginning at three months of age. All centers located in government-owned space must be accredited by the National Association for the Education of Young Children (NAEYC).

Federal child-care programs are attractive for many working parents, who can easily drop off and pick up children. In addition, they may be able to see their children during the workday. Most centers have an open drop-in policy, affording mothers the important opportunity to continue nursing after returning to work or allowing parents to spend their lunchtime or other free moments of the day with their children. This makes returning to work after maternity leave easier and provides some brief "quality time" with children for either parent.

3. Medical and Leave Benefits

The federal government offers employees and their families an excellent selection of health benefit plans that continue coverage through retirement. In addition, in 1993, Congress passed the Family and Medical Leave Act (FMLA). The FMLA allows employees to take up to 12 weeks of unpaid leave, without fear of losing their jobs, to care for themselves while ill or a newborn, adopted child, or sick family member. In 1999, recognizing that many employees could not take the needed leave because they could not afford to go without pay for that time period, the President issued a memorandum allowing federal employees to use up to 12 weeks of accrued sick leave each year to care for family members suffering a serious health condition.

D. IT'S NOT ALL ROSES: THE DISADVANTAGES OF FEDERAL EMPLOYMENT

One of the most obvious disadvantages of working in the public sector is the salaries, particularly when compared to private practice. As of summer 2000, large law firms in large cities were paying top lawyers at least two or three times the salaries paid to comparable government positions. In-house corporate law departments and smaller or less urban law firms have salaries closer to government pay, but still generally higher. This is not an issue just for those who want to become rich. Many lawyers have school debts and/or family responsibilities that put pressure on them to bring home more income than a government salary provides.

There are other disadvantages related to the work environment. Many government legal offices do not have enough competent paralegal and clerical support. In my office I have only one paralegal and two secretaries to support 13 lawyers—a ratio that might be considered unprofessional in private practice. Fortunately, technology increasingly mitigates the impact of sparse clerical support. Government office spaces are generally smaller and less attractively furnished than those in the private sector, and lawyers are more likely to have to share space. Office equipment such as computers may not be the most up to date and may be in limited supply. Generally, government travel rules require that transportation and accommodations expenses conform to a very tight budget, even on long, difficult trips or extended assignments away from the office. And of course, the government provides none of the special benefits found in the private sector, such as payment of bar association or club dues.

Unfortunately, the myth that government employees are incompetent or lazy may taint even the most professional and dedicated of government lawyers. This can make it hard to move into the private sector from a government job. Strict government ethics rules may limit mobility as well, at least for a certain time period. However, for many lawyers such disadvantages do not outweigh the advantages of public-sector employment. And in fact, the specialized and cutting-edge experience that public-sector international trade law lawyers acquire generally adds to their later marketability in the private sector.

E. OPPORTUNITIES IN THE FEDERAL GOVERNMENT

Department of Commerce. The Department of Commerce is probably the largest single employer of international trade lawyers in the United States. Of the several hundred lawyers at Commerce, about 100 focus on international trade–related issues, including foreign market access and development, trade agreement compliance, foreign investment, export licensing, antidumping duties, countervailing duties, intellectual property rights, product standards, technology, telecommunications, environment, and fisheries. A comprehensive description of the Commerce legal offices can be located at <http://www.ogc.doc.gov>.

Office of the United States Trade Representative (USTR). USTR is part of the Executive Office of the President. Approximately 20 lawyers at USTR provide advice on developing and coordinating U.S. international trade and investment policy, negotiating agreements with other countries on these matters, resolving disputes under these agreements and handling related legislative initiatives. (See <http://www.ustr.gov>.)

Department of Agriculture. Agriculture has many overseas programs involving development of foreign markets for agricultural products and negotiation of international agricultural trade agreements. The department's international lawyers provide legal advice to Agriculture officials on all these topics and work frequently with USTR. (See <http://www.usda.gov>.)

Department of State. The State Department's Office of Legal Advisor employs about 150 lawyers who provide advice on international legal issues. Most work on public international law, including foreign policy and national security matters, but some State Department lawyers specialize in trade and private international law and work frequently with Commerce and USTR. (See <http://www.state.gov>.)

United States Agency for International Development (USAID). USAID lawyers provide advice on foreign assistance and humanitarian aid programs. (See <http://www.usaid.gov>.)

Department of the Treasury. A number of lawyers at the Treasury Department provide legal advice on matters relating to international financial/monetary affairs, including international debt and taxation matters as well as customs, trade, and investment issues. (See <http://www.treas.gov>.)

Overseas Private Investment Corporation (OPIC). OPIC lawyers work on programs that provide loans, loan guarantees, and political risk insurance for investment projects in developing and transitional economies. (See <http://www.opic.gov>.)

Export-Import Bank of the United States (EXIM). EXIM lawyers advise on programs providing loans, loan guarantees, and export credit insurance to promote U.S. exports. (See <http://www.exim.gov>.)

The U.S. International Trade Commission (ITC). ITC lawyers support their agency's work as an independent, quasi-judicial federal agency that provides analytical trade expertise to both the legislative and executive branches of government, determines the impact of imports on U.S. industries, and directs actions against certain unfair trade practices, such as patent, trademark, and copyright infringement. (See <http://www.usitc.gov>.)

There are many other federal departments and independent agencies that hire lawyers who work on international aspects of their programs, including international trade or investment matters. A sample of these opportunities is listed below.

Department of Justice. The Justice Department has several offices employing international lawyers with such varying specialties as immigration law, foreign claims settlement, antitrust law, and other domestic criminal laws and federal programs with international implications. (See <http://www.usdoj.gov>.)

Environmental Protection Agency (EPA). The International Environmental Law Office in EPA's Office of General Counsel provides legal services in connection with the international aspects of EPA's environmental programs and also participates in the negotiation of international trade and investment agreements to ensure that environmental concerns are taken into account. (See <http://www.epa.gov>.)

Department of Labor. Certain international initiatives at the Department of Labor require legal advice. Labor lawyers often participate in negotiating international trade and investment agreements, particularly when immigration and worker rights are at issue. (See <http://www.dol.gov>.)

Food and Drug Administration (FDA). FDA lawyers engage in a number of international activities including the preparation of international agreements on product standards and scientific studies. (See <http://www.fda.gov>.)

The opportunities described above are only superficial summaries of the important work that awaits someone who practices international trade law in the public sector. When this work is joined with the balanced lifestyle generally possible in government employment, it makes for an exciting combination that should be considered by every young lawyer or law student interested in international law.

Practicing International Environmental Law: The Search for Green Pastures

10

by Daniel B. Magraw[1]

A. INTRODUCTION

International environmental law is relatively young, having been recognized as a branch of public international law only within the last 30 years. It is one of the most dynamic areas of international law. New international agreements, new institutions, new cases, and new "soft-law" instruments (for example, the annual declarations of the Commission on Sustainable Development) are constantly appearing. Even if the rate of change slows, the area will remain fluid, because the issues pertain to the integrity of the biosphere, human health, and the interface with economic and social policy.

The term "international environmental law" is used ambiguously by lawyers to describe both the practice of public international law relating to the environment and the practice of domestic law (U.S. or foreign) applicable to an international transaction, event, or dispute that involves a substantial environmental component. In the public international law sense, a practitioner must be expert in public international law and institutions, as well as familiar with

---

1. The views expressed herein are those of the author and do not necessarily reflect those of the U.S. government.

fundamental principles of environmental policy. In the domestic law sense, a practitioner must be expert in the relevant domestic environmental laws of the jurisdiction in which he or she practices, as well as conversant with principles of public international law generally and, more specifically, with any relevant international law, such as international economic law (especially trade law) and international dispute-settlement regimes. Because international environmental issues often involve scientific questions, lawyers who are "allergic" to science might well think twice about entering this field. Conversely, this field can be extraordinarily fascinating for lawyers who enjoy science.

In either the public international law or the domestic law sense, international environmental law is exciting and challenging. As international and domestic environmental regimes develop around the world and the amount of international trade and investment increases, economic transactions and disputes become increasingly intertwined with environmental issues, both international and domestic. International investment decisions must now take potential environmental liability explicitly into account. Moreover, environmental considerations (both procedural and substantive) now figure prominently in the decisions of international finance institutions (for example, the World Bank) and some export credit agencies (for example, the Overseas Private Investment Corporation and the U.S. Export-Import Bank). Similarly, international sales of goods are increasingly subject to health and safety regulations and import and export restrictions that are environmental in nature, as illustrated by the U.S. ban on importing shrimp caught without the use of turtle-excluding devices or food with residues of prohibited pesticides, and other countries' restrictions on importing genetically engineered organisms.

Environmental liability actions such as those generated by the Bhopal tragedy or by transboundary harm are likely to become more common. Moreover, domestic environmental regimes change as they mature—for example, as the United States introduces regulatory mechanisms based on economic incentives and reduces its reliance on so-called "command and control" approaches. This situation places a premium on foresight, adaptability, and creativity on the part of the international lawyer. Furthermore, many of the issues involved in environmental practice (whether purely domestic or international) have important public policy implications. They confront what may well be the most difficult intellectual challenge facing the world community—how to resolve the relationship between environmental protection and preservation on the one hand and economic activity on the other. Practitioners in this area thus frequently find that their work helps shape the policy debate and significantly influences society.

In sum, there is no question that international environmental law is an exciting, challenging, and important area.

B. WHERE INTERNATIONAL ENVIRONMENTAL LAWYERS PRACTICE

If one desires to practice international environmental law, where and how would one do it? The answers to these questions are not obvious, but it is easier to generalize about the "where." Essentially, international environmental lawyers may be found in seven sectors: law firms, corporations, academia (for example, law schools), consulting firms, environmental and business nongovernmental organizations (NGOs), governments, and international governmental organizations. Predictably, private practice (whether in law firms, corporations, or consulting firms) contains more of the domestic law type of international environmental law (although there is an increasing amount of counseling by private lawyers with respect to treaty negotiation and implementation). Legal work for business NGOs tends to have a more even split between public international law and domestic law practices. In the other sectors, the public international law aspect typically dominates international environmental practice. This does not mean, however, that there is a large number of lawyers whose practices contain a high percentage of international environmental law, either domestic or public. The supply of lawyers interested in practicing international environmental law exceeds the demand.

The question of how to find international environmental law work thus can be critical. It is related, of course, to the broader question of how to develop an international law practice of any type. For international environmental lawyers for whom a primary motive is to protect and preserve human health and the environment, however, there may be an ethical element not present in many other practice areas.

C. ADVICE FOR THOSE INTERESTED IN INTERNATIONAL ENVIRONMENTAL LAW

Law students who decide to prepare for a career in international environmental law would be well advised to take basic courses in public international law and domestic environmental law, followed by a course in international environmental law (if available). A course in conflicts of law also is highly advisable. More specialized courses might make sense if the student has a clear idea of which aspect of international environmental law he or she wishes to pursue, but some caution is in order. Interests often change. Practice opportunities in the chosen field may not arise, or other, more exciting possibilities may occur. And quite apart from those factors, the best approach often is to select elective courses on the basis of the professor's level of knowledge and ability to challenge his or her students.

Doing paid or volunteer work with an environmental NGO during law school can help establish one's "bona fides" with that community (which is so inundated with job applicants that it can be fairly demanding about such things), although any environmental legal experience would prove valuable in subsequent practice. Writing a law review piece on some international environmental law topic also demonstrates an interest and helps develop an expertise, although the quality of the piece and the venue of its publication often carry more weight than the topic. In any event, the experience of thoroughly researching a public international law subject is often invaluable.

Once out of law school, there are many things an aspiring international environmental lawyer can do to increase the odds of finding international environmental projects, including becoming active in professional organizations and writing articles. These are described elsewhere in this book, with the only real variation being the importance of establishing some connection with the public interest environmental community if one wants to work in that sector. However, as in all areas of the law, serendipity often plays a determining role in guiding lawyers to international environmental issues or cases.

D. FIRST EXPOSURE: OIL SPILL

My first exposure to international environmental law—other than in my public international law class in law school—came as an associate in private practice in Washington, D.C., when I was assigned to litigation involving damage to coastal fisheries and tourism from a major marine oil spill. Up to that point, I had worked quite hard to ensure that my practice had a dominant international law component through trying to do the best job I could, expressing my interest in international law, writing articles on international topics, and always being available to accept international work, regardless of how busy I was.

This assignment, which involved representing one of the alleged polluters, came from a partner for whom I had done a lot of other international law work. The work involved researching the applicability of an international liability convention and several questions of admiralty law. The case was fascinating and important, but at that juncture it seemed no different from any other major public international law case. Some of the other work I did with that partner involved international boundaries and their effects on resource allocation—another branch of public international environmental law. My experience practicing law in Washington, D.C., thus allowed me to work in pollution control and natural resource management—two of the three great branches of public international environmental law. I was not involved in any work on the third branch—cultural preservation.

My experience notwithstanding, most international environmental law found in private practice relates to the domestic law aspects described above. This work often interfaces with the public international law aspect of international environmental law, such as if the domestic law in question implements or is otherwise affected by an international environmental agreement (for example, the U.S. Endangered Species Act implements the Convention on International Trade in Endangered Species). As with other international law practice, the fun of working with other legal systems and with foreigners often is present. With the dramatic recent growth of international forums and agreements addressing environmental issues, opportunities for private-sector lawyers (both in-house and with firms) to advise clients on the negotiation and implementation of international agreements are expanding.

E. ADVANTAGES OF ACADEMIA

My permanent immersion into international environmental law occurred after I joined the law faculty at the University of Colorado, following private practice. It was more of a slide than a plunge. One of the great advantages of academia is the ability to choose the issues one thinks and writes about. I chose to write initially about general questions of state responsibility and international liability, which include questions of accountability for transboundary environmental damage. That work—which was not undertaken consciously because it involved environmental issues—led to writing a book chapter on the role of public international law in protecting U.S. national parks. This piece turned out to hold a special magic for me because of my love of the land and belief in the importance of protected areas. That realization, combined with ideas generated partly via those pieces, led to further work on international environmental protection, including several books and numerous articles.

I modified the curriculum of two of the courses I taught—Public International Law and International Development Policy and the Law—to include a greater environmental component. Such intra-course adjustments are relatively easy for professors to accomplish, partly because scholarship and teaching tend to be mutually reinforcing. Eventually I began teaching a course in international environmental law. My scholarly productivity in this area undoubtedly helped me obtain permission to include that course in the curriculum and in my teaching load, but I also was fortunate to have an understanding dean, cooperative colleagues, and overall curricular flexibility. In general, therefore, academia provides great opportunity to set one's own agenda (and to express oneself freely about the issues addressed), and I was able to develop my interest in international environmental law in that context.

I also did some consulting on international environmental issues while a professor. Although these were not wildly remunerative, they were very interesting and usually spiritually rewarding. Also, there is nothing like working on a few real-world problems to sharpen one's scholarship. My consulting work included such clients as the U.S. government on the international legality of a proposed coal mine in Canada that would have polluted the North Fork of the Flathead River, which forms the western border of Glacier National Park; a private company on a proposed chemical investment in India; and an environmental NGO on transboundary air pollution from smelters along the Mexico-U.S. border. Finding consulting work on such issues can be more difficult when one does not reside in Washington, D.C., but people and groups all over the country are interested in international environmental issues.

F. OPPORTUNITIES IN GOVERNMENT

In the U.S. government, many departments, agencies, and offices have lawyers who practice international environmental law. These include the Agency for International Development, Council on Environmental Quality, Department of Agriculture, Department of Defense, Department of Energy, Department of the Interior, Department of Justice, Department of State, Environmental Protection Agency (EPA), and the National Oceanic and Atmospheric Administration (Department of Commerce). When the interface between trade and environment is included, the Office of the U.S. Trade Representative, the Department of Treasury, the International Trade Commission, the Overseas Private Investment Corporation, and the International Trade Administration (Department of Commerce) must be added to the list. These and other U.S. government law offices are described from a more general perspective in "The Practice of International Trade Law in the Public Sector" chapter by Eleanor Roberts Lewis in this volume. Some of these agencies have specified international environmental legal staffs (for example, Department of State and EPA); others have lawyers who practice in the area but do not have official titles that indicate that fact. While the title is relatively unimportant, the absence of explicit international environmental responsibility in the title complicates the task of identifying the jobs.

Many congressional staff positions involve questions of international environmental law, some on a frequent basis. The Senate Foreign Relations Committee and the House Committee on Foreign Affairs are examples. The governments of border states such as California, Washington, and Texas also have lawyers who practice international environmental law.

G. EPA ACTIVITIES

The EPA provides an example of what international environmental work in the government can entail. The agency's international activities are extensive, reflecting the fact that domestic and international protection efforts have become inextricably intertwined. These activities include:

- Participating in negotiating international environmental agreements.
- Implementing international environmental agreements through domestic laws and regulations (for example, the Clean Air Act and regulations implement the Montreal Protocol on Depletion of the Ozone Layer and the U.S.-Canada Air Quality Agreement).
- Providing technical and other assistance (for example, to countries in Central America).
- Working on environmental issues along the U.S. borders (for example, on pollution of the Rio Grande and the Great Lakes).
- Analyzing the extraterritorial application of U.S. laws.
- Participating in policy-making on the interrelationship between international trade and environmental protection (for example, participating in conducting the environmental review and negotiation of the North American Free Trade Agreement).

EPA lawyers work on legal and policy issues raised by all of these activities, often working closely with lawyers from other parts of the U.S. government, particularly the Department of State's Office of the Legal Adviser.

H. NONGOVERNMENTAL ORGANIZATIONS

Due to the merger of domestic and international protection efforts, many environmental NGOs have staff who deal with international environmental legal issues. Examples of these include the Center for International Environmental Law, Environmental Defense, Environmental Law Institute, Greenpeace, Greater Yellowstone Coalition, Land and Water Fund, National Wildlife Federation, Natural Resources Defense Council, Public Citizen, Sierra Club, Sierra Club Legal Defense Fund, The Nature Conservancy, World Conservation Union (IUCN), World Resources Institute, and World Wildlife Fund. Some of the NGO work involves litigation, some involves foreign assistance, and some involves research; much involves advocacy in nonlitigation settings. The people tend to be unusually dynamic and the work very demanding, but rewarding.

I. INTERNATIONAL GOVERNMENTAL ORGANIZATIONS

Work in international governmental organizations also can be exciting. The legal staff of the United Nations Environment Programme (UNEP) does very important work, and lawyers work in UNEP offices in Nairobi and elsewhere. International environmental agreements often establish their own secretariats, which can involve novel and important legal work. The Basel Convention on the Control of Transboundary Movements of Hazardous Wastes and Their Disposal, for example, has a secretariat in Geneva. There are many others in other cities. Many other parts of the United Nations system, including the specialized agencies, engage in international environmental work of one sort or another, such as the Economic, Social, and Cultural Council; Food and Agricultural Organization; International Civil Aviation Organization; International Law Commission; International Maritime Organization; and the regional economic commissions. Consequently they have growing work portfolios for international environmental lawyers. Most of the lawyers in these organizations are not from the United States, but there is some room for U.S. lawyers, just as there sometimes is in institutions such as the European Union.

J. MULTILATERAL DEVELOPMENT INSTITUTIONS

The multilateral development institutions, such as the World Bank and the regional development banks, increasingly deal explicitly with environmental issues. This also is the case with international trade and investment organizations, such as the World Trade Organization. One may argue about how "green" these bodies have become; nevertheless, familiarity with environmental issues is now a regular dimension of legal practice there.

K. SUMMARY

In conclusion, there are several types of international environmental practice and many places in which to practice, but the supply of lawyers willing to do the work outstrips the demand. An aspiring international environmental lawyer often must exercise imagination and creativity just to find work in the area. But the work, once found, can be among the most dynamic and challenging, and sometimes spiritually rewarding, that the legal profession has to offer.

Seeking to Limit Suffering in Armed Conflict: The Work of an International Humanitarian Lawyer

11

by Louis Maresca[1]

A. INTRODUCTION

Afghanistan, Chechnya, the Democratic Republic of the Congo, East Timor, Rwanda, Sierra Leone, and the Balkans. These are just a few examples of the countries and regions that have experienced armed violence in recent years. Yet few people will have the chance to examine the events that occurred in these places in much detail. They are, however, places to which the practitioners of international humanitarian law pay particular attention. It is in these and other similar contexts where two seemingly opposing trends have collided: the large-scale use of armed force—more lethal today than at any other time in our history—and international efforts to minimize death and suffering in armed conflict. Far removed from the law library, the courtroom, and the judge's chambers, such places are the workshop of the international humanitarian lawyer.

This chapter provides an introduction to the work of an international humanitarian lawyer. It outlines the general

---

1. The views expressed in this article are those of the author and do not represent the views or position of the International Committee of the Red Cross.

tasks of the practitioner and some of the ups and downs of working at the international level to reduce the suffering that is all too prevalent in armed conflict today. It also describes how interested students can prepare themselves to pursue a career in this fascinating field. The perspective presented is limited to the work of an international humanitarian lawyer employed by an international or non-governmental organization.

B. WHAT IS INTERNATIONAL HUMANITARIAN LAW?

International humanitarian law is the branch of public international law that seeks to minimize suffering in armed conflict. It regulates, on the one hand, the conduct of warfare—that is, the weapons and methods that combatants are permitted to use in conflict to weaken or overpower an adversary. It also governs, on the other hand, the treatment of those who are not participating in the hostilities. Specifically, this means the wounded and sick, prisoners of war, and civilians. International humanitarian law seeks to ensure that force is directed only against legitimate military objects and to protect those who are unable to protect themselves or who may find themselves under the control of an adverse party. In short, it seeks to protect human dignity in situations of extreme violence.

C. TREATIES

The principal rules of international humanitarian law are found in international treaties, chiefly the Geneva Conventions of 1949 and their additional Protocols adopted in 1977.[2] The four 1949 Conventions are some of the most widely ratified treaties, accepted by nearly every country in the world. As of February 1, 2001, there were 189 states that are parties to each of the Conventions. The two additional Protocols of 1977 also have gained widespread adherence. As of February 1, 2001, 157 states have ratified additional Protocol I and 150 have ratified additional Protocol II.

---

2.   The full titles of the Conventions are: The *Geneva Convention for the Amelioration of the Condition of the Wounded and Sick in the Armed Forces in the Field; Geneva Convention for the Amelioration of the Condition of Wounded, Sick, and Shipwrecked Members of Armed Forces at Sea; Geneva Convention Relative to the Treatment of Prisoners of War; Geneva Convention Relative to the Protection of Civilian Persons in Time of War*. All four Conventions were adopted on August 12, 1949. The full titles of the 1977 Protocols are: *Protocol Additional to the Geneva Conventions of 12 August 1949, and Relating to the Protection of Victims of International Armed Conflicts (Protocol I); Protocol Additional to the Geneva Conventions of 12 August 1949, and Relating to the Protection of Victims of Non-International Armed Conflicts (Protocol II)*.

Many of the rules contained in these treaties are considered to be customary international law.

Other important international humanitarian law treaties include the Protocol for the Prohibition of the Use of Asphyxiating and Poisonous Gases and Bacteriological Methods of Warfare, the Convention for the Protection of Cultural Property in the Event of Armed Conflict, the United Nations Convention on Certain Conventional Weapons, and the Convention on the Prohibition of Anti-personnel Mines. Along with the Conventions of 1949 and their Protocols, these treaties establish the fundamental rules governing the conduct of war in both international armed conflict (war between states) and civil wars or similar conflicts within the borders of a single state.

While international treaties to minimize suffering in armed conflict are of fairly recent origin—the first was adopted in 1864—rules restricting the behavior of troops in combat have existed for nearly as long as recorded history. Many early religious and philosophical texts and other codes of conduct show that prisoners were not to be killed but taken and well treated; women, children, and the elderly were not to be targeted or harmed; and warriors were not to use barbarous weapons or methods of attack. Thus well before the development of international treaties, there was a long tradition in many cultures to limit the death, injury, and suffering caused by battle.

D. CHANGED NATURE OF WAR

Today, international humanitarian law is a detailed, comprehensive, and widely accepted body of law. Yet recent conflicts have shown that the nature of warfare has changed dramatically over the last several decades. Most wars now occur within the borders of a single state and involve national and international, state and nonstate actors. Many conflicts are unstructured, involving gangs of fighters accountable to no central authority and sometimes not fighting for any political, religious, or philosophical cause. Even when more traditionally structured conflicts break out, such as the Gulf War and the conflict in Kosovo, developments in tactics and weapons technology may have outpaced the state of the law. In light of such circumstances, ensuring that the object and purpose of the law are maintained and respected is the challenge facing the international community and those who work as international humanitarian lawyers.

E. INTERNATIONAL COMMITTEE OF THE RED CROSS

The International Committee of the Red Cross (ICRC) has a special role in the development and monitoring of international humanitarian law. The ICRC is an independent organization that is at the origin of the International Red Cross and Red Crescent Movement. It often is considered the "promoter and guardian" of international humanitarian law because it has historically played an important role in its development. Its founder, Henry Dunant, initiated the adoption of the first international humanitarian law treaty, the Geneva Convention for the Amelioration of the Condition of the Wounded in Armies in the Field, which was adopted in 1864. The ICRC also prepared the draft texts that were the basis for the negotiation of the Geneva Conventions of 1949, the additional Protocols of 1977, and several other international humanitarian law treaties and was given a mandate by the international community to monitor the application of the law in situations of armed conflict. Through its delegations around the world and its presence in nearly every armed conflict, the ICRC reminds and encourages combatants to respect their humanitarian law obligations. The ICRC is perhaps the only organization that deals with all of the various aspects of international humanitarian law at the international level.

F. THE WORK OF INTERNATIONAL HUMANITARIAN LAWYERS

International humanitarian lawyers are involved in the development, implementation, and monitoring of international humanitarian law. In short, they work to ensure that the law is being implemented by governments, respected by combatants, and is otherwise achieving its purpose in countries affected by conflict. On a day-to-day basis, such pursuits involve a wide range of interesting and diverse activities. Below is an overview of the primary tasks in which a practitioner of international humanitarian law may find himself or herself engaged.

- *Draft and negotiate international treaties.* International humanitarian lawyers are regularly involved in the drafting of new treaties or proposals to amend existing ones. They also are likely to assist in the diplomatic negotiations of final texts. In recent years the international community has been very active in promulgating new international humanitarian law instruments, particularly in relation to prohibitions on the use of certain kinds of weapons and the establishment of tribunals to prosecute violators. Treaties banning blinding laser weapons and antipersonnel mines were adopted in 1995 and 1997, respectively. Statutes for the international tribunals for the former Yugoslavia, Rwanda, and a permanent international criminal court, as well as a protocol for the protection of cultural property, also have been adopted in recent years.

- *Research the impact of armed conflict.* International humanitarian lawyers often author or contribute to reports examining the conduct and consequences of conflict. Research and analysis can shed light on general compliance with the law, identify lacunae, and contribute to the investigation of violations. Such studies are an important way to ensure that the law is achieving its objectives and are necessary for initiating international responses to new or outstanding problems.

- *Lobby governments to adhere to international humanitarian law treaties and develop and strengthen the law if necessary.* Practitioners of international humanitarian law work with states to facilitate their ratification of international humanitarian law treaties if they have not already done so. This often involves meetings with a range of government officials to inform them about the applicable law and provide assistance that will further the ratification process. They also consult with governments to promote the development or strengthening of the law if necessary.

- *Assist governments in the implementation of treaty obligations.* While international humanitarian law is applicable only in situations of armed conflict, ensuring that it will be applied once a conflict breaks out requires substantial preparation in times of peace. Examples of essential measures include work to ensure that the armed forces are trained to act in accordance with the law; preparations for marking of hospitals, medical units, and transports to ensure they are identifiable and will not be attacked; measures to identify and safeguard cultural property; the adoption of national legislation to prosecute violations; and the creation of review mechanisms to ensure that the development, production, or deployment of new weapons would not violate the existing law. International humanitarian lawyers work with governments to provide expertise on legal questions related to these and other areas and can furnish examples of steps taken by other countries in achieving these goals.

- *Monitor the application of international humanitarian law.* This work is particularly relevant in ongoing conflicts. Humanitarian organizations, and in particular the ICRC, frequently act in conflict situations, providing surgical, medical, and humanitarian assistance. Their presence provides their representatives with an opportunity to see that the law is being respected. While the ICRC generally takes a reticent approach, preferring, as a first step, to work bilaterally and confidentially with parties to a conflict, many nongovernmental organizations have now become active in this area and are much more outspoken when violations of the law occur. International humanitarian lawyers are asked to provide legal opinions on issues arising in such situations. These opinions are the basis for interventions with authorities in an effort to ensure respect for the law and demand an end to violations if the law is not being followed.

- *Follow developments in war-related technology and military doctrine.* The technological revolution affecting all aspects of daily life also affects the way modern war is waged. It is necessary to keep abreast of developments and ensure that the objects and purposes of international humanitarian law are not undermined in any way. Some current issues of concern include the development of new types of weapons (acoustic weapons, dazzling lasers, and other "nonlethal" weapons), attacks on computer networks as a method of warfare, a growing reliance on high-altitude bombings, and the widespread availability of small arms and light weapons.

- *Organize and participate in meetings, workshops, and briefings for government officials and others at the national, regional, and international levels.* Such meetings are intended to facilitate understanding of the law, increase adherence to the relevant treaties, promote its implementation, and address related issues and developments.

- *Author reports, publications, and texts in support of all the above activities.*

G. NONGOVERNMENTAL ORGANIZATIONS

For many years the above activities were primarily undertaken by international humanitarian lawyers working for governments, the International Committee of the Red Cross, universities, and research institutes. However, in recent years nongovernmental organizations have become very active in this domain. One well-known example is the Nobel Prize–winning International Campaign to Ban Landmines (ICBL), which, along with the ICRC, UN agencies, and other organizations, was the driving force behind the development and adoption of a treaty banning antipersonnel land mines. This coalition of some 1,300 nongovernmental organizations was instrumental in creating awareness about the problems caused by these weapons and in galvanizing public and political opinion in favor of a complete prohibition. This form of nongovernmental networking and coordination has begun to serve as an example. Nongovernmental organizations also played an important role in the development and adoption of the statute for the international criminal court and the protocol on the involvement of children in armed conflict. Many are now raising awareness about the consequences of the widespread availability of small arms and light weapons. It is likely that nongovernmental organizations will continue to play an important role in international humanitarian law and similar issues in the years to come.

This growing involvement in international humanitarian law issues by civil society has expanded the role of the international humanitarian lawyer. In particular, it has broadened the pool of contacts and working partners in all aspects of the law's development, universalization, implementation, and monitoring. Today, international humanitarian lawyers find themselves strategizing with organizations throughout the world. Greater public awareness also has garnered more media interest in legal issues. Thus, there is a growing need for studies, documents, and publications for non-expert audiences. In short, the development of the law is becoming a much greater part of the public discourse and the work that much more diverse, exciting, and challenging. Maintaining this widespread interest in international humanitarian law issues in light of the vast amounts of news and information competing for civil society's attention will certainly be a challenge for the future.

H. ADVANTAGES AND DISADVANTAGES OF THIS TYPE OF WORK

The range of activities of an international humanitarian lawyer certainly guarantees travel to fascinating places. There are trips to capitals to meet with government officials, representatives of civil society, and others involved in international humanitarian law. There also are trips to participate in international or regional conferences to promote development, adherence, and implementation of the law, as well as trips to conduct research on a range of related issues.

It is this opportunity to travel to war-torn countries that provides a unique aspect of being an international humanitarian lawyer. Witnessing firsthand the devastation inflicted upon towns and villages, meeting those who have lost limbs to antipersonnel mines, and speaking with people who have lost loved ones serve as a stark reminder of the human cost of every conflict. These are the personal memorials that every international humanitarian lawyer brings to his or her discussions in international conferences and government capitals.

Visits to countries affected by armed conflict also provide a rare chance to learn how the law fulfills (or not) its objectives. Outside the conflict, one hears very little about the instances when the civilian was not fired upon, when the child did not step on an antipersonnel mine because it had been removed, and when the sick, wounded, or captured were well treated by the adversary. Violations of the law certainly occur, and occur all too often. Yet there are many indications that the law is regularly followed and its objectives have been fulfilled. These visits provide an important confirmation as to why the application and implementation of this law is so important in today's world.

A practitioner of international humanitarian law is exposed to a wide range of issues. In addition to dealing with the conduct of war and how the wounded, prisoners of war, and civilians are to be treated, the law also crosses over into other fields such as disarmament law, human rights law, and refugee law. In addition, as international humanitarian law is directly linked with the existence of armed conflict, tangential issues of national, regional, and international security and international politics also lurk in the background. These factors make the work all the more interesting.

In light of the continued death, injury, suffering, and destruction occurring in armed conflicts today, perhaps the most frustrating aspect of being an international humanitarian lawyer is the slow pace of the law's development and implementation. Elaborating changes in international humanitarian law and ensuring their adoption and implementation can be a lengthy and bureaucratic process. Even when there is consensus that a problem exists and a will within the international community to address it, the development of new rules or alterations to existing treaties is likely to be preceded by years of expert meetings, formal and informal government consultations, and diplomatic negotiations. Similarly, even when a treaty has been adopted or amended, its ratification and implementation by governments may be unhurried. Thus, immediate results on the ground are often slow to materialize.

The development of a ban on antipersonnel mines may be a good example for the future. In addition to the unprecedented involvement of civil society in the development and implementation of the law, the speed with which a prohibition on these weapons traveled from a lofty idea to an international norm is striking. In less than five years, antipersonnel mines went from perceived as necessary weapons for national defense to weapons outlawed by two-thirds of the world's governments. The speed with which nations have sought to eliminate antipersonnel mines and bring relief to mine victims and mine-affected communities is equally impressive. Since the adoption of the Convention on the Prohibition of Antipersonnel Mines in 1997, the number of nations producing antipersonnel mines has dropped from 54 to 16, some 22 million antipersonnel mines in government stocks have been destroyed, and in 1999 alone over $250 million was allocated by governments to address the global land-mine problem. These are significant achievements that demonstrate that once a means of warfare has been stigmatized in the public conscience, steps to address the problem can be rapidly implemented.

I.   HOW CAN YOU PREPARE FOR A CAREER IN INTERNATIONAL HUMANITARIAN LAW?

Many of those who practice international humanitarian law also are involved in other areas of public international law. Lawyers working for nongovernmental organizations, for example, also may cover issues related to human rights law, disarmament law, or international criminal law. Nonetheless, students can take a number of steps to build a solid background in international humanitarian law and be prepared to work on humanitarian law issues.

1. Legal Studies

A solid legal education is perhaps the foremost requirement for the practice of any field of law at the international level. Studies in public international law, are particularly important, as the primary rules of international humanitarian law are found in international treaties and other sources of law, such as customary international law and the general principles of law. Thus, a good knowledge of the development and functioning of the international legal regime is a basic requirement.

The study of international humanitarian law itself is particularly useful. Yet very few law schools offer a specialized degree in this area. Most schools offer a general course as part of a specialization in human rights law, refugee law, or other similar field. However, even a general course related to the subject can provide an introduction to the law and a good foundation for further work and research. American University and the University of Essex are two schools that offer an advanced degree in international human rights and humanitarian law.

For those desiring more in-depth knowledge of international humanitarian law, the ICRC sponsors seminars for law students. These seminars provide an overview of the major treaties and themes of the law as well as more in-depth lectures on developments related to the law's application, implementation, and enforcement. Lectures are given by prominent practitioners and academics and offer a unique opportunity for advanced study and interaction with those who work in this field. Generally, a seminar for English-speaking students is offered every July in Warsaw. Summer courses for French- and Spanish-speaking students also are offered in other European countries. Further information about these seminars can be obtained from the ICRC or the National Red Cross or Red Crescent Society.

Whether one desires to work exclusively in international humanitarian law or in related fields, a good background knowledge, and even a specialization, in areas such as human rights law, disarmament law, and international criminal law also are beneficial. Today, many of the developments occurring in international humanitarian law intersect these subjects. Courses in comparative law also are a plus. A good knowledge of the major legal systems of the world can help in discussions with national authorities on adherence to the pertinent treaties and their implementation.

2. Overseas Experience and Language Skills

Work, study, and travel abroad are frequently perceived as important experiences for those wishing to work in any field of public international law. Such experiences are particularly important to organizations considering students or recent graduates for internships or other positions. They reflect a desire and an initiative to understand and interact with foreign people and cultures that, after all, is an important part of all international work. Exchange programs or extended study in European, Asian, or other foreign universities are useful ways to obtain such experience. They also can provide valuable opportunities to establish foreign contacts for further research and for those seeking internships or employment with organizations in other parts of the world.

The development of language skills is such an important point that it cannot be overemphasized. The ability to speak and write in two or more languages is a very useful skill that should be pursued. While English is certainly widely spoken within the international community and is the only language of many an international lawyer, the ability to work in other languages is widely respected. Language skills are taken into consideration by many organizations when recruiting interns or permanent employees. Which language you may want to study may depend on what region of the world you would like to work in, but, along with English, French and Spanish are widely used in international meetings. It is never too late to begin the study of a language. Even very basic comprehension and conversational skills are useful.

3. Internships

An internship with an international or nongovernmental organization is perhaps the best way to gain experience in the practice of international humanitarian law and thus facilitate continued work in this field. Many organizations have internship programs. As the "promoter and guardian" of international humanitarian law, internships with the ICRC provide unique opportunities to work on a wide range of issues in this area. National Red Cross and Red Crescent Societies also work on international humanitarian law issues. These should be the first stops for students interested in an internship or work in this field of law.

Internships also are available with the various agencies of the United Nations and its related organizations. While the United Nations does not have a department specifically dealing with international humanitarian law issues, a number of its agencies—the U.N. Department of Disarmament Affairs, the U.N. Center for Human Rights, and the U.N. High Commissioner for Refugees—are active in this field to the extent that the law intersects with their area of competence. The International Tribunal for the Former Yugoslavia and the International Tribunal for Rwanda also recruit interns and provide opportunities to research the many legal issues associated with the international prosecution for war crimes.

Nongovernmental organizations also offer internships that can provide exposure to the practice of international humanitarian law. Similar to the agencies of the United Nations, however, their sphere of activity often focuses on specific issues within international humanitarian law. The International Campaign to Ban Landmines, for example, concentrates on issues related to land mines—in particular, the universalization and implementation of the Convention on the Prohibition of Antipersonnel Mines. Once again, nongovernmental organizations dealing with issues related to human rights, disarmament, refugees, and international criminal law are likely to welcome interns and have certain aspects of their work touch upon international humanitarian law issues.

Keep in mind that the application process for internship positions with the ICRC, the United Nations, and other international organizations can be fairly competitive. Each year the number of applications far exceeds the number of available positions. Yet, even if a student is unsuccessful through the normal application process, he or she often can obtain an internship with an idea for a specific research project that would be valuable to the organization. New issues or legal developments that may have an impact on the operations or mandate of an organization are the most likely to garner serious consideration. Such ad hoc internships can provide valuable exposure in the organization that may lead to further work on other projects.

4. Networking

Obtaining internships or research projects is as much a matter of luck as it is ability and experience. Being in the right place at the right time or having someone remember your name are just as likely to lead to a phone call inviting you in for further discussion as going through a formal application process or a mass-mailing of your curriculum vitae. Thus, networking can be valuable. Conferences and seminars are particularly good venues to initiate contact with practitioners. A number of these meetings touching on international humanitarian law issues are organized each year by universities, research institutes, and international law societies. Interested students should attend such events and speak with international humanitarian lawyers about related legal issues and possible topics for further research projects.

J. CLOSING THOUGHTS

This chapter has provided an overview of the work of an international humanitarian lawyer. It is an interesting, diverse, and dynamic profession with travel to fascinating places, rich interaction with foreign people and cultures, and the chance to obtain a unique and firsthand perspective on what is happening in so many parts of the world today. While this body of law is limited to situations of armed conflict, it is, of course, a part of the larger efforts to protect human dignity in all situations and in all parts of the world.

Thus, it is an immensely satisfying occupation on both the professional and personal levels. Working in this field certainly requires a commitment to humanitarian issues— one may never enjoy a large salary, a Christmas bonus, or business or first-class travel. Nonetheless, enjoying and believing in the substance and purpose of one's work are benefits of immeasurable value in and of themselves.

Fair Winds and Following Seas: A Career in Admiralty Practice

12

by Michael Marks Cohen

A. INTRODUCTION

Admiralty is the granddaddy of all international commercial law, with antecedents that stretch back to Biblical times. For more than 500 years there have been written maritime codes covering carriage of goods by sea, general average, salvage, marine insurance, seamen's rights, and arbitration. In the absence of statutes, judge-made rules have been applied to collision, shipboard personal injury, carriage of passengers, shipbuilding, ship finance, and ship chartering. In modern times, these traditional subjects have been supplemented by shipping regulation and water pollution. Although now there are many treaties and much local legislation, the courts continue to play a very active role in shaping the law to changing circumstances.

Like 60–70 percent of my generation, I was drawn to the admiralty bar by seagoing experiences, having served for three years as a naval officer on a destroyer in between college and law school at Columbia. At the time, many individuals opted for naval or Coast Guard service rather than be drafted into the Army during the period between the Korean and Vietnam wars. One consideration was to parlay our legal training and military experience into a career so we could put our time in the service to good use. After clerking for Stanley H. Fuld, the chief judge of the New York Court of Appeals, I started out in maritime practice as a trial lawyer with the Admiralty & Shipping Section of the U.S. Department of Justice in Washington, D.C. Three years later I came to Burlingham Underwood and have been in the firm ever since.

Admiralty principles and concepts are generally similar throughout the world. In many respects, maritime law is a sort of written and unwritten uniform commercial code that has been adopted by each country with local variations. Foreign precedents—especially English ones—are frequently cited and are regarded as very persuasive. There is a good deal of maritime litigation in the United States, mostly in the federal courts, since federal law is controlling. Generally, apart from personal injury cases there are no jury trials.

Maritime law strives for uniformity. New developments are, therefore, followed not just locally but nationally. Moreover, it is the only area of federal law where older cases are commonly more highly regarded than more recent ones, partly because maritime matters formed such a substantial part of the work of the Supreme Court up until just after World War I. A remarkable number of current procedures in federal civil litigation, which are intended to promote fairness and simplicity, have their origin in admiralty practice—some of it more than 150 years old and/or of foreign derivation. Routinely, many disputes are not taken to court at all but instead are voluntarily submitted to arbitration in London or New York, often before commercial arbitrators rather than lawyers.

B. DISADVANTAGES

There are a few disadvantages in admiralty practice. Most cases involve claims under $250,000; few go as high as $10 million. Such blockbusters as the *Titanic, Andrea Doria, Amoco Cadiz,* and *Exxon Valdez* come along only once every decade or so. Hardly ever is there a case that will make or break the client. While world events have an immediate impact on the day-to-day practice, in reality, shipping involves the legs rather than the heart of world trade.

Compensation is adequate but not fabulous. Much of the work comes from a comparatively small number of marine insurance companies, a situation that fosters price competition. In addition, the nature of the work makes it difficult to leverage—that is, to put more than one associate on a case with a partner. These factors force admiralty lawyer income levels below those of colleagues in other fields.

Shipping is not an explosively expanding field. Moreover, it is susceptible to large cyclical swings. Very few new domestic shipping companies are formed. Established companies do not change legal advisers very often. Most new clients are referrals from existing clients, or from local corporate law firms, or from out-of-state or foreign admiralty lawyers.

C. ADVANTAGES

For all of that, there are quite a number of advantages to the practice. Because of the historical role of London in marine insurance, salvage, ship finance, and ship chartering, all admiralty lawyers and their clients throughout the world speak English. It is not necessary to be fluent in a foreign language to have a successful practice and a rewarding career.

The bar is small—almost a craft guild—with only a few thousand full-time practitioners here and abroad. Frequent contacts among the lawyers are maintained across state lines and international boundaries. Locally, in the cities where they practice, admiralty lawyers have a well-deserved reputation for professionalism and courtesy in their relations with one another. There are several unusually active national and international bar associations. The number of maritime lawyers practicing together in a firm is usually small. In New York, many of the maritime firms concentrate on shipping law, with perhaps some additional work in aviation and the sale of bulk commodities that are shipped by sea, such as oil, grain, and sugar. A few New York firms, and one or two others elsewhere in the country, may have as many as two dozen admiralty partners and associates. But for the most part, there are usually fewer than ten maritime lawyers in any given firm. In major port cities, those lawyers can sometimes be found as a small department of a large corporate law firm.

There are frequent opportunities for travel to interesting places—most often London, Tokyo, and Hong Kong. Clients tend to be very practical, often colorful figures. The risks in shipping appeal to individuals who enjoy gambling for high gains in a short period. The sums can be large. Time differences, geographical separation, weather uncertainties, human errors, and the need for quick decisions call for analytical skills and imaginative tactics that are not usually found in a nonmaritime commercial practice. It is definitely not a stuffy field.

Practice is very closely tied to the headlines in the newspapers. Natural disasters such as earthquakes and hurricanes, as well as predictable seasonal events, such as ice in the Great Lakes, promptly cause clients to seek advice. The same is true for world events—war in the Persian Gulf, pirates off Singapore, refugees fleeing in small boats at sea, the decline of the dollar, turmoil in South America. When combined with individual calamities—groundings, oil pollution, boiler breakdown, pilfered liquor, rotting fruit, leaking holds—the work can indeed be very stimulating. It is not only intellectually challenging but fast-moving: lawyers are commonly called for spot advice while a crisis is in progress.

But the overall lifestyle in maritime practice is generally much more relaxed than large corporate work. Time can usually be found for bar association efforts, writing for professional journals, and, most important of all, being with family. Practicing admiralty law ought not to destroy your marriage or ruin your children.

In recent years a very high percentage of associates joining admiralty firms have been women. There is widespread religious diversity at the bar. Greater racial diversity would be welcome.

D. TRAINING

Although not essential, an admiralty course in law school would be helpful, not only for careers in practice but also for those seeking clerkships with federal judges in port cities. Experience at sea with the Navy, Coast Guard, or Merchant Marine is useful but, again, not a prerequisite. Perhaps the best training for admiralty practice is to write an article on a maritime law subject for a student journal in law school.

E. STARTING OUT

A good place to start out is the Torts Branch of the U.S. Department of Justice. Nearly all admiralty cases involving the federal government are handled centrally by about 24 admiralty lawyers in Washington, D.C., New York, and San Francisco. There are a few openings annually.

In private practice, New York is by far the biggest market. There are new jobs for perhaps two dozen associates with maritime firms there each year. Outside New York, all the major seaports, the Great Lakes, and the inland rivers combined may produce an equal number of openings.

Firms can be difficult to locate just through Martindale-Hubbell. All firms that have at least one MLA member are listed, however, in the directory of the Maritime Law Association of the United States (MLA) at its Web site, <www.mlaus.org>.

My Career as a Latin-American Transactional Lawyer

13

by Andrew J. Markus

A. INTRODUCTION

As I approach my 25th year in the practice of law in law firms, I can now reflect on what it is to be an international lawyer, and particularly one focused on mergers and acquisitions and other transactions in Latin America. I wrote a chapter, "Miami International Practice," for the first edition of *Careers in International Law* in 1993. Looking back at that chapter, it appears to me that many of my reflections are still valid and appropriate. However, I have quite a different perspective on the practice of law, given the great advances in technology that have occurred in the past eight years. I would therefore like to relate how I became an international lawyer, what it is like to practice law in a law firm, what it is like to undertake Latin-American mergers and acquisitions, and what you can do to pursue a career in international law.

B. WHY I BECAME AN INTERNATIONAL LAWYER

I became a lawyer, naturally enough, because I had an early interest in the law. I remember reading a book, *So You Want to Be a Lawyer*, when I was in seventh grade. Whatever that book said to me, it must have been powerful because here I am, all these years later, a practicing lawyer. To be fair, my father also helped me become the business lawyer I am today. He was a businessman and exposed me to a wide variety of U.S. businesses. After that, I knew that the only kind of lawyer I wanted to be was a business lawyer.

So why did I then become an international business lawyer? Sometimes—and I think this happens more often than not—people find their special talents by accident. That was certainly what happened to me. My special talent is an ability to relate to things international. I became aware that I had a natural affinity toward the cultural aspects of international matters and that I related well to individuals from other cultures as a result of my travels in Europe in the summer of 1970. Travel was an eye-opening experience for me. I knew then that I was born to be international. I was going to law school. So I aimed to make myself an international lawyer.

Little did I appreciate the long and interesting path I had chosen.

C. LAW FIRM PRACTICE

How does talking about what it is like to practice in a law firm pertain to your path to international law practice? Well, let's assume that you are at the beginning, or nearly the beginning, of your career path as you read this chapter. As important as knowing that you want to do something international in the law is the environment from which you attempt to do it. This is important for several reasons:

- As a lawyer, you will be hired by a client for your legal skills. If you do not have top-of-the-line training, it is just that much harder to be a good lawyer. It will not serve you well to be a culturally aware lawyer if you cannot lawyer your way out of a paper bag.
- It is always easier to swim downstream. If you are fortunate enough to be hired and trained by a great law firm, you will have many more options in the future than if you start by hanging out your own shingle.
- If you practice law in an environment in which anything international is met with incomprehension, your international aspirations will wither and die unless you change to an environment that is supportive.

What big firms generally offer that small firms do not is the luxury of training and the opportunity to work on large transactions. You may not feel that this is a luxury at 11 p.m. while you work on reviewing due diligence or drafting an agreement for the client to review the next morning, but you will find, in hindsight, that you have learned much and, in fact, have an edge on most of your contemporaries. Large transactions bring into play all the skills that are required to do smaller transactions properly, but your firm can bill for these services and therefore has the luxury of allowing you to be on the team.

To be hired by a large, prestigious law firm in the United States, you must apply for and be accepted to do a summer clerkship at the firm. The lesson here is: plan early. Many a third- or fourth-year law student has approached me about becoming an associate in my firm. Invariably, they have been too late. With some foresight, that tardy law student could have been taking his or her place in the class of associates from which tomorrow's best international lawyers will come.

What small firms offer that big firms do not is hands-on experience at an early age. However seductive this may be, delay this gratification until you have received a good grounding in your chosen discipline. While there are exceptions, often small firms do not provide a viable platform for high-level international corporate work. On the other hand, small firms do provide a lawyer with the ability to handle a client's transaction from beginning to end and to be responsible for it. They also provide young lawyers with the opportunity (a mixed blessing, to be sure) to generate their own clients.

Medium-size firms (by that I mean firms with 20 to 100 lawyers) seem to have the disadvantages of both large and small firms. The medium-size firm often does not provide hands-on experience at an early age or a viable platform for high-level international corporate work. It also does not provide a young lawyer with the opportunity to generate his or her own business. The trend appears to be toward medium-size firms, and even firms that would qualify in my numbering system as large (those with more than 100 to about 400 lawyers) are dissolving or being acquired at an accelerating rate. Thus, in the future, it may be that there are two types of law firms—the mega firm and the small boutique firm.

D. WHAT DOES A LATIN-AMERICAN TRANSACTIONAL LAWYER DO?

My son has asked me what I do all day. Do I buy and sell Latin-American companies? Sometimes directly, and sometimes indirectly. Do I practice foreign (non-U.S.) law? No. Most often, I am engaged in the practice of U.S. law with non-U.S. aspects. For instance, if I am engaged in an asset acquisition in which many of the assets are non-U.S. companies or operations, many issues arise under foreign law. The framework of my agreement, however, is U.S. (typically New York or Delaware) law. The entities involved are typically New York or Delaware corporations or other entities. Therefore, for instance, if some of the assets are in a Brazilian *limitada*, questions as to title to the assets, rights attributable to the assets, and the like are certainly governed by Brazilian law. Do I opine as to these aspects? No. Local counsel is an absolute necessity in this circumstance and plays a key role in the validity of such an acquisition.

If, on the other hand, I am engaged in a merger, it is generally of U.S. entities with operations in Latin America. In this type of transaction, usually many more issues of U.S. law present themselves than issues of foreign law. One thing is virtually certain: the U.S. entities' operations will be accomplished by a number of Latin-American entities. However, the transaction is rarely positioned so that mergers between the in-country entities form the transaction. Generally, the transaction takes place at a level in which defined commercial law such as that of New York or Delaware may govern and in which the courts of New York or Delaware or an international arbitral tribunal can have jurisdiction. Thus, once again I am a U.S. lawyer practicing U.S. law with international aspects.

E. HOW YOU CAN PURSUE A CAREER IN INTERNATIONAL LAW

My thoughts on this matter are strictly U.S.-oriented. I have practiced in large and small firms, in my own firms, in other people's self-made firms, and in old established firms. Whatever else they have in common, for an international lawyer, the environment of the firm is the most important thing to consider. If the firm does not have a commitment to international practice, spend your time getting the best domestic law education you can and plan to move in a few years when you have a good basic knowledge of what it is like to be a first-class lawyer.

Another aspect to consider on the path to "internationaldom" is that law firms are, at their essence, businesses. The exigencies of businesses often demand that their employees take paths different from those envisioned by them or the firm. This realization came to me one day when, having been hired to do international things in a law firm, I found myself doing real estate finance and development work instead. It was not what I was suited to do. It was not what I had planned to do. It was not even what my law firm planned that I do. But it was what there was to do. I used the experience to make myself more of a well-rounded lawyer. But I never forgot what I wanted to do with my career.

As it became apparent that my international opportunity was not going to occur in that firm, I did what is now commonplace—I changed firms. I did not move to a new firm for the money. My inducement was that the new opportunity would bring me closer to my career goal. That framework for viewing my career has led me to make several more changes in my career path. I practice now in Miami as one of the senior members of the Latin-American practice group of a well-known, well-regarded New York law firm doing corporate work such as mergers and acquisitions for Latin Americans and Europeans in the United States and for U.S. and non-U.S. companies in Latin America.

I learned several lessons:

- *First, be clear about what you want to do.* Try to really feel certain internally and try not to fool yourself about your desires. You may find that you really don't want to be a lawyer at all, but a businessperson, an artist, or a writer. Or maybe (God forbid) you want to be a trial lawyer. One thing is evident to me: if you aren't clear with yourself, you will find yourself moving in directions that you don't understand.
- *Second, use what you learn, wherever and however you learn it, to further your chosen direction.* I could have been a real estate lawyer representing large institutions in complex real estate lending transactions or representing developers building large projects. Instead, in my early career, I took my good domestic law skills and applied them to representing non-U.S. investors and financiers of real estate projects. From there I developed relationships and gained experience in the transactional aspects of business representation. My clients started doing things other than real estate or introduced

me to others who did things other than real estate. I factored all these learning elements into my chosen direction and eventually began to do complex mergers and acquisitions domestically and internationally.

- *Third, develop relationships early and often.* I have heard it said that the seeds for business one plants as a lawyer often take a long time to germinate. What is true is that your friends will be the ones to send you business and help you develop future contacts. As a young lawyer, your friends will generally not be in a position to help you (or you, them) at the start. Be patient and keep contact with your friends. They are your future.

Finally, do not despair if the job that you find initially does not appear to be international in scope. Just remember to keep focused on what you want to do as you go along and look for an opportunity to do it. Keep your eye on where you want to go and not where you are coming from. Assuming you still want to be an international lawyer, move in that direction. I do not think it is heresy anymore to suggest that you may need to move from one firm to a number of different firms before you feel that you are doing what you want to do. You might not make it on your first, second, or even third move, but do not despair. Keep your proverbial eye on what you want and you will achieve it.

Practicing International Criminal Law

14

by Daryl A. Mundis*

A. INTRODUCTION

On July 7, 2000, Duško Sikirica, a former police officer in Prijedor, Bosnia and Herzegovina, entered pleas of not guilty to two counts of genocide, three counts of crimes against humanity, and two counts of violations of the laws or customs of war for his alleged role as commander of the Keraterm prison camp in northwestern Bosnia and Herzegovina. Although not a senior-level political leader in the conflict that consumed the former Yugoslavia in the early 1990s, Sikirica—who appeared in court with his arm in a sling and with a broken nose, both allegedly inflicted when elite British troops snatched him from his home in the early morning of June 25, 2000—is allegedly one of countless other individuals who turned on their neighbors to kill or drive them away. He will have his day in court, judged by the international community for his role in a conflict that the Security Council deemed to be such a threat to international peace and security that an international criminal tribunal was established to try those responsible for serious violations of international humanitarian law in the

---

* The views expressed here are solely those of the author and are not to be imputed to the United Nations or the International Criminal Tribunal for former Yugoslavia.

former Yugoslavia. I will be one of the prosecutors trying the case against Sikirica.

B. THE EMERGING INTERNATIONAL CRIMINAL LAW SYSTEM

As recently as a decade ago, there were virtually no full-time practitioners of international criminal law. This is not to imply that lawyers were not engaged in transnational criminal matters, such as extradition or the occasional high-profile trial of individuals charged with acts of international terrorism or drug trafficking. But from the post–World War II Nuremberg and Tokyo trials until the establishment of the International Criminal Tribunal for the former Yugoslavia (ICTY) in 1993 or the International Criminal Tribunal for Rwanda (ICTR) in 1994, there were no international courts trying individuals alleged to have committed grave breaches of international law.

More recent developments suggest that international criminal law will continue to expand in the next few years and may well be the largest growth area for careers in public international law. For example, it is likely that the International Criminal Court (ICC) will be established within a few years, although the United States is unlikely to be a party to that court. As of mid-2000, discussions were under way in the Security Council for establishing an ad hoc tribunal for offenses allegedly committed in Sierra Leone. United Nations officials and Cambodian government leaders are negotiating to establish a similar tribunal for 1970s offenses committed by the Khmer Rouge regime. The United States is financing a London-based nongovernmental organization seeking to establish a tribunal to try Saddam Hussein and other Iraqi officials for crimes against humanity and other serious breaches in Iraq. An ad hoc tribunal was considered but ultimately rejected in East Timor to try those responsible for violations of international humanitarian law in the late 1990s on that territory. Rather, such violations are being prosecuted in local courts with the assistance of the international community.

It is still too early to tell if any of these efforts will actually result in the establishment of additional international criminal tribunals. However, the fact that the ICC will have prospective jurisdiction only means that until the ICC is established, the international community will have two choices when faced with serious breaches of international humanitarian law: creating additional ad hoc tribunals or allowing those suspected of committing such offenses to go unpunished.

This chapter will explore opportunities and suggest possible directions for careers in this burgeoning field. At the outset, two important points should be kept in mind. First, the developing system of international criminal justice is focused on several core crimes: genocide, crimes against humanity, war crimes, and the still undefined crime of aggression. The delegates who negotiated the Treaty of Rome establishing the ICC intentionally disregarded other serious international crimes, such as drug trafficking, terrorism, and money laundering, preferring to leave the prosecution of such crimes to national authorities. Second, there are career opportunities in federal and state court systems for individuals interested in these types of crime, although few government offices have large staffs devoted to prosecuting such crimes. Such opportunities are beyond the scope of this chapter.

The existing ad hoc international criminal tribunals (the ICTY and ICTR) are the primary focus in this chapter, since they are currently the only existing institutions and will probably serve as the model for any future ad hoc tribunals. The types of career opportunities that will be available at the ICC are still an open question, but it is unlikely they will deviate substantially from the practice and organizational structure of the ad hoc tribunals.

C. THE STRUCTURE OF THE ICTY AND THE FUNCTIONS OF ITS LAWYERS

Pursuant to the statutes of both the ICTY and ICTR, they are composed of three organs—Chambers, Registry, and the Office of the Prosecutor (OTP). Both the Registry and the OTP employ a substantial number of lawyers. The Chambers technically consist of the judges only; the lawyers who support the judges are staff members of the Registry. Although the two tribunals share a common basic structure (with minor differences), the discussion that follows is based on the ICTY.

As organs of the Security Council, the ICTY and ICTR follow the personnel policies of the United Nations; consequently, lawyers at the tribunals hold several different titles, based on experience and staffing requirements. Senior legal officers (or, in the OTP, senior trial lawyers) generally possess at least 12 years of professional experience. Legal officers generally have at least eight years of professional experience, while associate legal officers must usually have a minimum of three years. In the current structure, neither ad hoc tribunal has any positions at the assistant legal officer level (entry-level legal positions).

1. Chambers

Trials before the ad hoc tribunals are conducted without juries before trial chambers consisting of three judges, no two of whom are from the same country. Both tribunals have three trial chambers. In addition, there is a five-judge appeals chamber that both tribunals share as a means of harmonizing the jurisprudence of the tribunals. Each judge is assigned one associate legal officer, and each chamber as a whole has two associate legal officers, one legal officer, and one senior legal officer (two for the appeals chamber). Thus, the Chambers Legal Support Unit (of the Registry) has about 32 lawyers.

These lawyers perform a variety of functions and tasks that are similar to the duties of law clerks in the U.S. system. This system is based more on the European model, whereby "clerking" for a judge may be a lifelong career. The senior legal officers thus have a great deal of responsibility and perform a variety of functions, such as overseeing depositions. More junior lawyers undertake legal research and assist with the drafting of orders, decisions, and judgments.

2. Registry

The Registry, which provides administrative support to the ad hoc tribunals, employs about a dozen lawyers who work on a variety of issues, including enforcement of sentences, relations between the tribunal and the host state, and other matters of general international law. The Registry has three lawyers assigned to the Office of Legal Aid, which administers the provision of high-quality legal representation to indigent accused and assists defense counsel with administrative matters. Finally, the Registry has one lawyer assigned to the Office of Public Information Services to assist with legal queries from the media and the public.

3. OTP

The Office of the Prosecutor employs the largest number of lawyers at both ad hoc tribunals. Under the current structure, there is one prosecutor for both the ICTY and ICTR. She has one deputy prosecutor responsible for each tribunal. As with the common appeals chamber, this structure permits greater harmonization between the prosecutorial policies at both ad hoc tribunals.

The OTP has approximately 60 lawyers in The Hague. As in many national police forces (such as the F.B.I.), a significant number of the investigators have law degrees, although technically they are not working as lawyers, hence their role in the prosecution of cases will not be discussed further. The OTP is composed of two primary divisions, prosecutions and investigations, with several smaller units, such as the legal advisory section and the appeals section.

Prosecutions. The prosecution division consists of about 50 trial lawyers, who are allocated to two functional sections: the trial section and the team legal officer and co-counsel units. Eight senior trial lawyers, each assisted by a trial section legal officer, form the backbone of the trial section. These lawyers are responsible for prosecuting cases, with the assistance of lawyers from the team legal officer and co-counsel units. As a general rule, the trial section legal officers assist the senior trial lawyers with written pleadings and drafting motions and responses to defense motions, although those with advocacy experience may appear and examine and cross-examine witnesses.

Investigations. While the trial section lawyers spend the bulk of their time in court, moving from one case to the next as the cases are ready for trial, the team legal officers and lawyers from the co-counsel unit work closely with the investigators to develop the cases and move them through the pretrial stage. Once the accused is in custody and the trial chamber places the case on the docket, these lawyers assume the role of co-counsel, working directly under the supervision of the senior trial lawyer assigned to the case. These lawyers must be skilled at providing succinct yet accurate legal advice on investigative matters, including search-and-seizure issues. They also must be experienced in the art of questioning witnesses and victims and interrogating the accused. In short, the senior trial lawyers are highly experienced criminal litigators and the co-counsel are experts on the case to be tried, based on their long experience in working with the evidence and witnesses throughout the period of investigation and pretrial workup.

Legal Advisory Section and Appeals Unit. The legal advisory section, which consists of eight lawyers, provides critical support with respect to substantive issues of international humanitarian law and comparative legal analysis. The appeals unit, consisting of six lawyers, handles all legal issues arising during the course of either interlocutory appeals or appeals on the merits. Lawyers from both of these sections must have very strong research and writing skills, as well as a thorough knowledge of the applicable substantive and procedural law.

4. Defense Counsel

Finally, of course, the practice of international criminal law also includes defense counsel. Pursuant to Article 21(4)(d) of the ICTY Statute, the accused has an absolute right to counsel of his or her own choosing. In the event the accused is unable to afford counsel, he or she is provided legal assistance at no cost to him or her. The Registry maintains a list of defense counsel eligible for assignment to defend indigent accused. Moreover, the lawyer must speak at least one of the two official languages of the tribunal (English or French) and must be willing to be assigned to represent any indigent suspect or accused. A lawyer who does not speak one of the official languages but speaks the native language of the suspect or accused may be admitted to the list at the request of a suspect or accused where the interests of justice so demand. Under the relevant directives on the assignment of counsel, an indigent accused also may be entitled to co-counsel and an investigator at no cost.

D. THE PROS AND CONS OF LIFE INSIDE THE ICTY

Numerous professional and personal benefits arise from practicing international criminal law, particularly the opportunity for professional growth. This is the cutting edge of the law and provides endless opportunities to deal with issues of first impression, necessitating creative lawyering and problem-solving. Because the Rules of Procedure and Evidence are a unique hybrid of common law and civil traditions, practice before the ad hoc tribunals presents educational challenges, forcing the practitioner to look at the law from different perspectives. Also, because we rely to a greater extent than most national systems on a comparative approach to the law, there are ample opportunities to learn about foreign criminal procedure.

From a personal point of view, most of us take great pride in the importance of the work we pursue. It is immensely gratifying to be a small part of reconciling the parties to the conflict in the former Yugoslavia, and working with victims and witnesses can be empowering. Most of us truly enjoy working in a multicultural institution, where a majority of the world's states is represented. There are travel opportunities for interviewing witnesses and collecting evidence. And the benefits package is quite generous, although of course it cannot really be compared to the financial rewards of practicing with a big law firm.

These same advantages present certain drawbacks. Practicing international criminal law is not for the faint of heart. By definition, the crimes that are prosecuted at the ad hoc tribunals are serious and often involve mass killings, rape, and other offenses involving multiple victims—not exactly topics of pleasant dinner conversation with a spouse or significant other. Working on the same case day in and day out for months on end can take a psychological toll. As is the case with other types of litigation, the hours can be quite long, particularly during trial. Although it is exciting at first, many lawyers grow weary of the frequent travel necessary to interview witnesses, gather evidence, and visit crime scenes. While it may seem exotic to travel to distant lands in search of the truth, the fact is that many lawyers quickly tire of the substandard accommodations and lack of infrastructure that are all too common in areas that are regularly visited. Finally, although the financial rewards are generous, they are significantly less than what an experienced litigator could earn in private practice. In fact, starting salaries for first-year associates with major New York firms are higher than the salaries earned by senior legal officers and trial lawyers at the ad hoc tribunals. All of these factors can take a toll on practitioners with families who may not fully appreciate the personal sacrifices required in this type of work.

Balancing the pros and cons, it is clear that international criminal practice may not be for everyone. However, this type of work can be quite addictive.

E. SOME PRACTICAL ADVICE FOR LAW STUDENTS

My own experience may be helpful to students contemplating a career in international criminal law. As an undergraduate, I studied international relations and Russian, which included a summer abroad in the Soviet Union. Once in law school, I studied international law as my primary focus but also took as many courses in criminal law and procedure as my law school offered. While at law school I joined several groups, including the American Society of International Law and Amnesty International. After passing the bar, I joined the U.S. Navy and was a criminal litigator for nearly six years, including two and a half years in a foreign country.

Following my discharge, I decided to pursue an LL.M. in international law. While studying, I attended as many conferences as possible, always bringing copies of my résumé with me. While attending one such conference, I made an effort to meet ICTY President Gabrielle Kirk McDonald. After exchanging pleasantries, she asked for a copy of my résumé, which I readily provided. Within a few months, and before I actually received the LL.M., I accepted a position in President McDonald's Chambers. When she retired from the ICTY 18 months later, I accepted a position with the ICTY Office of the Prosecutor, where I am now on the team prosecuting Duško Sikirica.

There are as many routes into this career path as there are people practicing this type of law. However, all the international criminal lawyers that I have known have one thing in common: they all took full advantage of every opportunity that came their way. Those serious about a job in this area must maintain their focus on that goal and work to make it happen. The following are a few pointers that should help.

1. Law School

Many law schools today provide a wide range of international law subjects, and presumably anyone interested in a career in international criminal law would find many of these courses interesting. Other law schools, however, offer only an introductory course on international law, and a few do not even offer the basic course. The degree to which your law school offers courses in international law need not be a deterrent for your successful entry into this field, however, because the best advice for anyone contemplating a career in international criminal law is solid performance in law school.

Learning the basic skills necessary to be a good lawyer is essential for anyone aspiring to a career in international criminal law. This means learning to write clearly and succinctly, to spot and address issues, and to develop and frame an argument. Good research and advocacy skills—both oral and written—also are crucial. Participation in many moot courts or trial advocacy courses is a good idea. Joining the staff of an international or comparative law journal or submitting a note for publication also are wise moves.

All law students interested in this field should take the "full package" of courses available to all students interested in pursuing a career in criminal litigation. This includes criminal law, criminal procedure, and evidence. Advanced courses in due process or rights of the accused also should be taken, if possible. Choice of courses in law school should include international law, human rights law, and comparative law. Advanced courses or seminars in international humanitarian law, international criminal law, or similar courses should be taken if available.

2. Graduate School

Once the basics have been mastered, returning to law school to pursue an advanced degree may be a good idea. Earning an advanced law degree, such as the Masters of Law (LL.M.) in international law or even international criminal law, may be very helpful to those interested in a career in international criminal law and provide an edge over the competition. As previously discussed, the ad hoc tribunals have subject-matter jurisdiction over genocide, crimes against humanity, and violations of the laws or customs of war. Law school criminal law classes typically do not cover these offenses, and an understanding of the basics of these crimes will undoubtedly assist you in the process of job-hunting in this field. Although some of the lawyers in the OTP lack this formal educational training, many others have earned such degrees, and, given the stiff competition for positions, the more formal education you possess, the stronger your chances of being hired.

In many countries, students pursue the Bachelor of Laws (LL.B.) degree as the first college degree out of high school. Thus, unlike their U.S. counterparts, the first law degree is not something that is pursued after the completion of a basic undergraduate degree. Many of these students then pursue a specialized LL.M. in international law immediately after graduation from college, then go on to earn doctorates in international law before entering the job market. Due in part to this difference in how lawyers are trained throughout the world, an advanced law degree may be helpful in landing the position desired.

Many law schools offer an LL.M. in international law and a few even offer a highly specialized LL.M. in international criminal law. Such training will prove invaluable as you master the substantive law necessary to be an effective international criminal litigator. Moreover, many of the faculties offering advanced law degrees in international criminal law are located overseas, such as in the United Kingdom or the Netherlands. By pursuing such a degree program, you can also take advantage of studying and living abroad.

3. Study or Living Abroad

Many law schools and other higher-education institutions offer summer, semester, and/or year abroad programs. These should be seriously considered, since they offer the opportunity to learn about new legal cultures and languages. Study abroad programs also are great ways to meet other students with similar interests. The friendships and connections made during the course of such programs may last a lifetime.

4. Practical Experience

Because there are few, if any, entry-level positions in this career field, the best career advice is to gain as much criminal or appellate litigation experience as possible. The strongest candidates are those with excellent oral and written advocacy skills and the ability to work closely with investigators in developing a case. Good written and spoken communications skills are essential, as is the ability to analyze complex factual situations. Trials at the ad hoc tribunals tend to be rather lengthy, with numerous exhibits and witnesses. For example, the Blaškić trial lasted for 25 months. In terms of complexity and length of trial, the closest analogy to domestic trials is probably a prosecution under the RICO statute.

Virtually all lawyers practicing international criminal law began their careers practicing criminal law in their national jurisdictions. The skills learned as a young lawyer in the office of the local district attorney or U.S. attorney are invaluable. Young lawyers in such offices are exposed to what criminal practice is all about and usually are assigned a large number of cases, forcing them to juggle many legal issues simultaneously. The procedural issues that are confronted—evidentiary matters, due process problems, search-and-seizure issues, and substantive legal questions—are crucial training for any lawyer who wants to pursue a career in international criminal law.

Working in a foreign country and in a multicultural environment with people from different legal backgrounds is enjoyable. Because teams of lawyers work on all cases, the ability to work closely with others and respect their point of view is a definite asset. Finally, a keen awareness of current events in the world is a big plus. The headlines of a conflict in a far-off land today may be the bread-and-butter of a lawyer's practice tomorrow.

5. Internships

There are several internships that may lead to full-time paid positions in international criminal law. For example, interns generally perform substantive legal work in all three organs of both ad hoc tribunals. However, there are slight drawbacks to these programs. First, they are unpaid and generally require a commitment of four to six months. Second, the intern is forbidden under UN regulations from applying for a paid position for six months following the end of the internship. Thus, more than one year will elapse between the commencement of the internship and any resulting paid employment. Third, because law students from many countries also apply, the competition consists of students who have already completed their LL.M. (and may be working on their Ph.D.). Nevertheless, an internship can be a very rewarding experience, and, for most interns, the experience confirms that the practice of international criminal law is what they want to pursue.

6. Language Training

Both ad hoc tribunals use English and French as their official languages, although the witnesses are likely to speak Bosnian/Croatian/Serbian (at the ICTY) or Kinyarwanda (at the ICTR). The ICC, however, will use the official languages of the United Nations (Arabic, Chinese, English, French, Russian, and Spanish), and witnesses appearing before that court are likely to speak a wide range of languages. Thus, it is difficult to determine which language is the most likely to help you get the position you want.

Unless one has a gift for languages, is very diligent in language studies, or has the opportunity to live or study abroad for a considerable period of time, fluency in a foreign language will probably not be achieved. Do not let this deter you from making the effort to learn a new language, however. Learning a foreign language has numerous benefits and will always open doors for the student who takes full advantage of the opportunity. In addition to promoting cross-cultural communication, language skills help develop different ways of thinking and provide an edge in a competitive environment.

7. Networking

Opportunities abound for networking with professionals in the field and this may be an important means of learning of job openings. Given the sharp rise in interest in international criminal law, there are typically panels on the subject at most annual meetings of professional groups. For example, the ABA's Section of International Law and Practice, the American Society of International Law, and the International Association of Prosecutors typically offer panels and discussion groups addressing these issues during their regular meetings. The ABA Section of International Law and Practice has several committees for individuals interested in a career in international criminal law, including the International Criminal Law Committee and the International Courts Committee. Several nongovernmental organizations, such as Amnesty International, Human Rights Watch, and the Lawyers Committee for Human Rights, also are quite active in issues that interest practicing international criminal lawyers. Joining such organizations and actively participating in their meetings will provide a familiarity with the key players in the field. The publications of and internship opportunities in such organizations also can be helpful to those who would like to pursue a career in international criminal law.

F. SUMMING IT ALL UP

The challenges of working in the dynamic area of international criminal law are great and the rewards are even greater. However, the work is not easy and, frankly, can be depressing at times, since it focuses on some of the evil acts of humanity. Dealing with victims and criminals day in and day out can be emotionally draining. For example, more than one witness at the ICTY has directly appealed to one or more of the accused with the simple question, "Where did you bury my son?" Nevertheless, most of us engaged in this line of work take a great deal of pride and satisfaction in knowing that our work is of great importance to victims and their families, witnesses, and the international community as a whole. If we can play a small role in reconciling past international conflicts—and deterring future atrocities—then that is a true privilege.

Life in Paris: An Expatriate's Story

15

by Salli A. Swartz

A. INTRODUCTION

I never wanted to be a lawyer. However, parental influence led me to put off my fledgling career as an actress to attend law school. I always had an interest in international affairs, and spent my junior year of college at the Sorbonne and the prestigious Institut des Etudes de Science Politique in Paris. However, I came to international law in a fairly roundabout manner.

Once in law school, and after experiencing the political upheavals of the late 1960s and early 1970s in America and France, I wanted to change society and help the world. Although I did take all of the international law classes that my law school offered and obtained a certificate in international law, I did not take any of the courses that would have prepared me for a career in corporate law—an unwise move. It occurred to me only much later in my career that a competent international lawyer must have a firm foundation in U.S. corporate law.

I began my legal career as a legal service lawyer in rural Pennsylvania and practiced poverty law. For three very productive, constructive, and educational years, I represented abused spouses, the homeless, and welfare recipients, and even had the thrilling experience of pleading a welfare case before the Supreme Court. I was directly responsible for a full caseload, assisted clients directly, pleaded in all levels of the courts, and quickly became a hands-on, full-fledged lawyer. I found the practice of poverty law totally fulfilling, primarily because I believed that I was doing something constructive to help society.

However, personal circumstances intervened.

B. HOW I GOT TO WHERE I AM

I decided to accompany my French husband to Paris, where he was posted for an envisioned term of 18 months. After six months, his promised position in the United States did not materialize, and we decided to stay in Paris. With my average law school grades from a "close to Ivy League" law school and my background in poverty law, I was not a plausible candidate for either the New York firms with offices in Paris or French law firms: first, I was American with no name value on my résumé; second, I was a woman.

I sent out more than 100 résumés before and after my arrival in Paris. International organizations such as UNESCO bypassed me, perhaps because I was American (that is, I did not fall within the proscribed quota). I could not practice poverty law because I was not and could not become admitted to practice law as an *avocat* (see below). Moreover, there was no profession of poverty lawyer as such, since all French *avocats* are required to represent the indigent in civil and criminal proceedings and are paid directly by the state. I interviewed with some corporate firms but that was ultimately unsuccessful.

Knowing that I needed to get in the door, I accepted a job as an international arbitration paralegal at a salary significantly less than the managing partner's secretary's salary. Several months later, I was, however, promoted to lawyer status, and 18 months thereafter I was admitted to practice as a foreign *conseil juridique* (similar to solicitors in England).

At the time, to be admitted to the list of foreign lawyers, one needed a proven record of at least three years of experience (including 18 months with a firm in Paris), as well as an amazing amount of paperwork. Once these tasks were accomplished and my file duly examined, I was admitted to practice as a foreign lawyer.

I stayed with that firm for several years and received unique and incomparable experience in international arbitration. However, after spending the better part of four years working essentially on two very complex turnkey construction arbitrations in the Middle East, I wanted to gain a more diverse experience in French law.

Once in the door with "proper" credentials in hand, it was easier for me to find my second job. I decided I should move to a French firm with an international practice so that I could learn French law and become operational as a French lawyer, and improve my language and drafting skills. When making the move, I confronted another problem: the French firm was a firm of *avocats* (similar to barristers in England). *Avocats* had a monopoly on access to most of the French courts, but their practice was and is not confined only to pleading. In addition, *avocats* could not employ *conseil juridiques.* To become an *avocat* at the time, you needed to have French nationality and pass an exam, neither of which I intended to do; therefore, I was back to the nonstatus of a salaried employee having legal credentials but not officially admitted to practice law in France.

My experience with the French firm was interesting and certainly a worthwhile and necessary stepping-stone. It afforded me the opportunity to learn the ropes, and I gained the self-confidence that is crucial for living and working in a foreign country. But it could not be my final destination because it had a major downside: since I was not officially admitted, I could not become a partner.

After four years, I felt it was time to move on, which I did when I received an offer from a subsidiary of one of the then "Big 6" accounting firms. Aside from the fact that I could become an official foreign *conseil juridique* again, this job was essentially a learning experience that permitted me to determine what I did not want to do. I disliked accounting for every second of my time and getting a "report card" every Friday afternoon (work-in-progress, billables, and so on)—I felt guilty all weekend. I did not find that the client matters were significantly more interesting than those with which I had dealt in my prior two firms. But mostly, I found that I did not like the bureaucracy and politics of big firms.

After only one year of my "Big 6" experience, one of my French colleagues passed the exam to become an *avocat* and asked if I would be interested in starting a firm with her. My first reaction was disbelief: I had no clients and no idea how to attract them. My second reaction was to say yes.

Consequently, in 1988 two women—one French, one foreign, one an *avocat,* one a *conseil juridique*—started an international business law firm in Paris. The word from the lawyers with whom I had previously practiced was that we would fold in six months. In fact, I had secured our first client on an annual retainer before we rented office space, and the amount of the retainer was sufficient to pay overhead for the first year. We started drawing a salary after only two months.

After two years, we moved to bigger premises and joined forces with three other lawyers. The firm grew slowly but surely; we were not interested in growth for growth's sake. With our past experience in large firms, we were more inclined to keep our practice small and friendly. Then my original partner decided to change tracks and joined a family-owned business. Partially as a consequence of her leaving and partially because I felt that there was insufficient professional growth potential with the other lawyers at my firm, I made the difficult decision to "break up" the firm I had started. I then joined another firm in Paris as a lateral and name partner and brought with me my loyal team of players.

C. WHAT I LIKE AND DISLIKE ABOUT MY JOB

I have never been more pleased with my professional situation. In my opinion, I have all the advantages of working in a high-powered international law firm, but few of the disadvantages that accompany a partnership in a big firm. Once I decided that I did not want to practice in a large organization, the type of practice I developed was more a function of the clients who trusted me with their business projects than my choice of practice areas.

My current practice is quite diverse by choice, which has both advantages and disadvantages. Because I quickly become bored without a constant diet of challenging work, I decided that the most fulfilling situation for me was not to become specialized in any particular aspect of international business law but rather to go where my clients wanted to take me.

Since I started my firm in 1988, I have dealt with industrial and intellectual joint ventures in such countries as France, India, Poland, and Qatar, and negotiated the purchase, lease, and financing of aircraft and the granting of hydrocarbon exploration and exploitation rights for several Middle-Eastern and African governments to different international consortiums. On behalf of my U.S. and English multinational clients, I have created companies in France, acted as general counsel to those companies, and advised on labor law, commercial leases, and commercial contract negotiations and terminations, such as distribution, agency, IP technology transfers, and other types of commercial endeavors.

On behalf of my French clients, I have assisted in acquiring and divesting businesses and companies in England, France, the Netherlands, other European countries, and the United States. Due to my common-law training and background, they often come to me for help in understanding U.S. laws and regulations, such as export controls and the Foreign Corrupt Practices Act (FCPA). I also have assisted the heads of governments and royal families in acquiring real estate in France. That is always nice for a change of pace, since shopping for chateaux is hardly a disagreeable experience.

More recently, I have acquired several French and Spanish start-ups as clients and advised them on French and European Internet law, privacy regulations, competition issues, and intellectual property problems, such as the crossroads between trademarks and domain names and ownership of Web sites and Web site software. I also advise a major French telecommunications company in connection with the spinoffs of start-ups using knowledge developed by the telecommunications company and have represented major (and minor) U.S. software companies in connection with the licensing of their proprietary products to French companies.

The downside of this type of "generalist" practice is that it can be rather stressful on occasions. It can sometimes mean that you are learning frantically about a subject in a compressed period of time, although the stress often produces an excellent work product. Being a jack-of-all-trades in a small- to medium-size firm also means doing a bit of everything, including proofreading, research, photocopying, coffee making, and calling your own taxi at 10 p.m. But it also means less politics and fewer power struggles among the lawyers and staff.

D. ADVICE FOR LAW STUDENTS

1. Choosing the Right Job

The choice of jobs is more a lifestyle choice, since there are small boutique firms that are highly specialized in certain practice areas and those that are not. Consequently, my advice on choosing the type of firm is based more on the atmosphere than on the type of substantive practice.

Some lawyers take to large institutions like ducks to water, while others prefer a smaller, more intimate pond. The real trick in finding a fulfilling job is not the name on the door or even necessarily the type of law you think you want to practice, but the structure and atmosphere of the firm, company, or institution. You may tire of the subject matter, but the atmosphere will be permanently draining if you are not suited to it. It is worthwhile to obtain as much experience as you can in different legal positions so that you will be equipped to decide what type of organization best suits your personality, temperament, and goals.

2. Choosing to Be an Expatriate

Being an expatriate is not easy. It requires a firm vision of what you want to do, who you are, and the type of expatriate you think you want to be.

There are those who barely learn the language and spend their free time in American clubs socializing with Americans. Some attempt to lose their American identity as quickly as possible and try to blend in (this is usually fairly impossible to achieve if you have not been raised in the country). And then there are those of us who are probably somewhere in between, who enjoy becoming familiar with the language and culture, but who also are very much at home with their American background and culture.

Practicing law as an expatriate complicates matters, since you will find yourself applying your Americanized reasoning and drafting techniques to a culture that may or may not value such techniques. I spend a great deal of time explaining the business, financial, legal, and cultural environment in France to my U.S. clients so they can develop constructive working relationships with their local management—not always an easy task, given the different manners in which the two cultures deal with professional differences.

I also am called upon to explain the business, legal, financial, and cultural environment of the United States to my French clients, discussing such matters as the history and importance of the Foreign Corrupt Practices Act (FCPA) and the manner in which Americans negotiate deals. More important, I spend a great deal of time explaining one culture to the other in the hope that the cultural issues, once clarified, will enable the two sides to concentrate on the business issues.

As an expatriate dealing in several different cultural environments (yours, your client's, and the other side, for example), you must be constantly on guard—watching for reactions, anticipating them, and explaining them. Business negotiations in a multicultural situation are quite challenging, because what you see and hear does not always have the same significance that you may assume it does. You must be in a position to analyze your own cultural prejudices and set them aside, then be aware of what is occurring and not occurring so that you can explain the situation to your client and the other party without giving the impression that you are taking sides.

You need to be flexible, which means you can understand a position taken by a party without adopting it as your own position. You are, in essence, a cultural mediator at the same time you are an advocate for your client. This situation is not only baffling during the first few years, particularly if your language skills are uncertain, but can be perilous if you are not totally aware of the cultural particularities of the parties who are negotiating the deal. It is quite a tightrope to walk.

The job also is very challenging and fun ... which is why I am still practicing law in Paris today.

Perspectives of an Academic International Lawyer

16

by Mark W. Janis

A. INTRODUCTION

Perhaps the best proof that international law is "real" law is the fact that there are so many international lawyers. Thousands of practitioners worldwide call themselves international lawyers. More than 10,000 are members of the Section of International Law and Practice of the ABA. To a considerable degree, international law is the practice of the international lawyers of the Section and everywhere.

It has been my pleasure to chair the ABA International Law and Practice Section's Committee on the Law of the Sea and now its International Legal Education Committee. For six years, I was privileged to serve on the Section's governing council, playing a small part when the ABA created the Central and East European Law Initiative (CEELI), a remarkably fruitful innovation. I also have edited the Section's two books, *Careers in International Law,* the first published in 1993, the second this 2001 publication, happily co-edited with Salli Swartz, both of us ably assisted by Beth Foxwell.

The practice of international lawyers is changing in myriad ways. This is a practice I initially saw in the 1970s, first when a law student at Oxford and Harvard and then for three years as an associate of Sullivan & Cromwell in New York and Paris. Two decades have been added as an international law teacher and writer, mostly at Connecticut and Oxford, but also for short times at Aix-Marseille, Cornell, Paris, and UCLA. By now, many of my students have themselves become successful international lawyers. It is good to see three of the University of Connecticut Law School's lawyers on the pages herein: Steve Glick in London, Cliff Hendel in Madrid, and Lou Maresca in Geneva. Of course, I have come to know many other international lawyers, not only at my professional and academic venues, but by working alongside them for many years in the U.S. societies for international law: our own ABA Section of International Law and Practice, the American Society of International Law, the International Law Association (American Branch), and the International Law Section of the Association of American Law Schools.

As I look at the practice of international lawyers, what strikes me most is how dramatically our profession has changed over 30 years, especially in the eight years between the first and second edition of this book. To tell this story, let me succinctly (much more has been discussed in the other chapters) discuss seven important changes in international lawyering from the perspective of an academic international lawyer:

1. Improvements in pre-legal international education
2. Improvements in international legal education
3. The ubiquity of the international LL.M. degree
4. More diverse employment opportunities in international law
5. Developments in international legal research
6. The transformation of the means of communication
7. The accelerating pace of international legal work

B. IMPROVEMENTS IN PRE-LEGAL INTERNATIONAL EDUCATION

Although it is often lamented that Americans are relatively poorly equipped with foreign languages and intercultural skills, I find this complaint groundless, at least looking at new U.S. law school students. Ever-increasing numbers of incoming U.S. law students are already very well educated in foreign languages and foreign culture. They are more ready than ever before to cope with the complexities of international transactions, and the quality of pre-legal international education keeps improving.

Much of the credit must go to the proliferation of college year and semester abroad programs. A great many law students nowadays have studied extensively overseas and honed at least one language pretty thoroughly—often Spanish, French, German, Russian, or Chinese. Moreover, college courses, not only in foreign languages but also in foreign history, politics, and society, are more plentiful both in the United States and abroad. The independent international studies and researches that many of our students have done while undergraduates are also quite impressive. Before they reach law school, many of our students are already comfortable in a foreign setting.

As a former high school exchange student to the Netherlands and a Rhodes scholar who took an English law degree at Oxford, I can testify to the invaluable advantages of international study. I am convinced that skills in foreign languages and foreign cultures pay real dividends for young U.S. lawyers, not only in finding places at law schools but in getting good jobs and beginning a successful international legal practice. Twenty years ago one often heard older U.S. lawyers say that the English language and a background in U.S. law and culture was all they ever needed for international transactions. That was, however, often defensive and never actually true. Such boasts are virtually never heard now. The quality of the international background of our newer international lawyers is simply too strong and the competition on the playing field of international transactions too intense for U.S. international lawyers even to pretend that an adequate background in foreign languages and societies is not essential.

C. IMPROVEMENTS IN INTERNATIONAL LEGAL EDUCATION

If anything, improvements in international legal education have been even more dramatic over the past few decades than international education gains at the undergraduate level. Law school curricula typically used to include a basic course in international law and perhaps an additional offering or two in international business transactions, international tax, or comparative law. My own law school "diet" at Harvard was heavy on business and financial courses. Nowadays, however, many law schools also provide courses in subjects as diverse as international trade law, international human rights law, international environmental law, the law of the European Union, international commercial law, international financial law, and international arbitration and litigation. Rather than one or two professors with an international law or comparative law expertise, there are often five or six on many law school faculties.

International opportunities in law schools have expanded not only in the classroom but also in extracurricular activities. There used to be only a handful of student international law journals; now there are more than 50. Thousands of young lawyers have had the advantage of editing and writing about international law before ever going into practice. The Jessup Moot Court competition is as active as ever. There are international law society speakers and conferences.

Also important are the more than 100 overseas summer law programs that offer different international courses and new international law professors, many of them foreign, to law school students. There also are increasing numbers of exchange programs with foreign law schools offered during the regular academic year, giving young U.S. lawyers the chance to witness foreign legal systems firsthand. For my part, I have had some administrative success in organizing student and faculty exchanges between Connecticut and Oxford and law schools in France, the Netherlands, Italy, and China, and in helping law school students initiate and run several conferences both at home and abroad.

D. THE UBIQUITY OF THE INTERNATIONAL LL.M. DEGREE

Another development on the educational front is the ubiquity of the LL.M. degree, not only for foreign lawyers studying in the United States, but also for U.S. lawyers studying overseas. After completing law studies in one's own country, the value of spending an additional academic year studying law in a foreign country and, often, in a foreign language attracts thousands of young international lawyers every year. There are now more than 50 ABA-accredited LL.M. programs for foreign law graduates in the United States, and many more programs exist for foreign lawyers, including U.S. lawyers, overseas. Although I did not take an LL.M. (I completed the regular law courses both at Oxford and Harvard), I have had a hand in administering graduate law programs at both Connecticut and Oxford.

I can attest that there is really no substitute for these popular LL.M. programs. They provide a uniquely accessible opportunity to better the cross-cultural understandings so critical for a successful international legal practice. If the course is taught in a foreign language (and English is the foreign language for most international LL.M. students in the United States), improving that language is a valuable bonus. Ordinarily the complaint about these one-year LL.M. programs is that "the time went by too quickly," a complaint rarely uttered about the basic law degree program in the United States or elsewhere.

E. MORE DIVERSE EMPLOYMENT OPPORTUNITIES IN INTERNATIONAL LAW

It used to be that the ordinary first job for a U.S. law student interested in becoming an international lawyer was with a large private law firm, often in New York or Washington, D.C. Indeed, this was the route I chose, practicing with Sullivan & Cromwell first in New York and then in Paris. My first law job, like the first international law job for many, would either develop into an international lawyering career itself or would serve as a stepping-stone for an international law opportunity with another employer. More often than not, it was impossible for students to find a first law job with an international aspect; one had to wait for the second or third job for that prospect.

Nowadays, it is easier to find international lawyering jobs at the outset of one's career, because there are more of them. Many smaller U.S. law firms and many law firms outside New York and Washington now offer international opportunities. Moreover, there is a range of other possible initial employers: foreign law firms, U.S. and foreign corporations, international accounting firms, public and private international institutions. This range of opportunities becomes even greater for those who have completed an LL.M. at a foreign law school.

My own career path turned to academic international lawyering. This field too has experienced growth. Most of the nearly 200 ABA-accredited law schools have increased their international law faculties in the last several decades. They recruit at an annual Association of American Law Schools hiring conference. Good grades, some writing experience, and a few years of practice or clerking are ideal qualities for the prospective academic international lawyer. There also are opportunities for academic international lawyers in graduate and undergraduate schools of government and political science and business schools. For many, the non–law school academic environment may be preferable, but for me the law schools provide a happy mix of the theoretical and the practical. In this, my 21st year of law school teaching, I enjoy teaching public international law and international business transactions (and the occasional "domestic" course, such as constitutional law), and working not only with the literature of the law but with the law students who will become lawyers and, indeed, with the many practicing lawyers. There is, I think, a bright future for academic international lawyers. Law student and lawyerly interest in international subjects is great and increasing. As political, economic, and social transactions become increasingly international, there should be a greater number of useful roles for international legal academics to play as teachers and scholars.

F. DEVELOPMENTS IN INTERNATIONAL LEGAL RESEARCH

Reading and writing about international law is what I like best about my job, although teaching comes a close second. Probably no aspect of the international legal profession has changed so much over 30 years as international legal research. It used to be that significant international legal research could be conducted only in a handful of major law libraries, mostly in principal cities or universities. Nowadays, computer-based research has placed a wealth of international legal resources in the hands of practitioners anywhere hooked up to the World Wide Web. It is possible to research a vast number of foreign and international legal issues literally anywhere. A lawyer in the smallest town in America can read cases, statutes, and doctrine from foreign countries and international sources just as easily as a practitioner in New York or Boston.

The ease of finding foreign and international sources has not, however, made the work of the international lawyer less time-consuming. The materials uncovered with the aid of the computer must still be read and analyzed. Indeed, the improvements in international databases have only added to the workload in many transactions.

As the method of research has changed, so has the method of delivery to readers. Traditionally printed books now vie with e-books, audiobooks, those on CD-ROM, or some combination of these formats. My seven books on international law, including *An Introduction to International Law* and *International Law Cases and Commentary*, may one day appear in an unexpected venue or be downloaded quickly and easily from the Internet.

G. THE TRANSFORMATION OF THE MEANS OF COMMUNICATION

Computers, of course, have not only transformed legal research, they have transformed the very practice of international law. There used to be time lags of several days or a week between posting a letter giving legal advice or a legal document and its receipt, and then another space of time for a client's or another lawyer's response to be posted and received. In the past three decades, communications have improved dramatically, first with the fax machine and then with the Web. Now, not only can information reach recipients more or less immediately, but many more recipients can be included. As with legal research, these technological advances have only made for more work. Not only are responses expected more quickly, more individuals have been woven into transactions.

H. THE ACCELERATING PACE OF INTERNATIONAL LEGAL WORK

Thus, the quickening of communications is accompanied by acceleration in the pace of international legal work. International lawyering was probably never leisurely, but it has never been as hectic as is today. International lawyers, like other lawyers, are always on call. Given a worldwide practice, there is never a time when many international transactions "sleep." And as the transactions stay awake, so the international lawyers are awakened, kept incredibly busy in the midst of potential 24-hour workdays.

Add to this the amount of travel required of international lawyers, and the job is more taxing than most other sorts of legal careers. It used to be thought that improved communications—not only fax and e-mail but teleconferencing—would make face-to-face meetings less essential, but this has not proved true. Clients and transactions still insist on the lawyer "being there," and so "there" the lawyers are. And those lawyers are no longer able to focus on a single transaction when away from the office. New means of communication have enabled them to stay looped into other transactions even while traveling. As an academic international lawyer, I am thankful to be able to set my own agenda, rather than have my agenda set by clients.

I. CONCLUSION

There are more and more international lawyers. Ours is a growth industry. The reasons are not hard to find. Increasing numbers of international transactions—commercial, financial, and governmental—have made more work for international lawyers. As always, international transactions, with their mix of languages, laws, and cultures, need more lawyering than garden-variety domestic transactions. So an increasing multitude of legally demanding international transactions call forth an increasing number of international law jobs, many of which have been described in this volume.

Appendix A
ABA-Approved Foreign Summer Programs, 2000

Editors' note: At press time, the list of ABA-approved foreign summer programs for 2001 was not yet available. For the most recent list, visit <http://www.abanet.org/legaled/studyabroad/abroad.html> on the World Wide Web.

U.S. Law School	Location of Program	Dates
1. Alabama Box 870382 Tuscaloosa, AL 35487-0382 www.law.ua.edu	Fribourg, Switzerland	May 16-June 16
2. American 4400 Massachusetts Ave NW DJLS/SPA, Ward Circle Bldg 244 Washington, DC 20016-8043 www.wcl.american.edu	Paris, France Geneva, Switzerland	June 8-July 8
3. American	Santiago, Chile	May 28-July 5
4. Arkansas-Little Rock/Baltimore UALR School of Law, 1201 McAlmont St Little Rock, AR 72202 www.ualr.edu/~lawschool	Haifa, Israel	June 29-August 8
5. Baltimore/Univ of Maryland Univ of Baltimore School of Law 1415 Maryland Ave, Baltimore, MD 21201 law.ubalt.edu	Aberdeen, Scotland	June 19-July 28
6. Baylor PO Box 97288, Waco, TX 76798 law.baylor.edu	Guadalajara, Mexico	July 30-August 13

U.S. Law School	Location of Program	Dates
7. Brooklyn/Loyola-Los Angeles Summer Prgms Abroad, Loyola Law School 919 S Albany St Los Angeles, CA 90015 www.brooklaw.edu/school	Beijing, People's Republic of China	July 23-August 5
8. Brooklyn/Loyola-Los Angeles	Bologna, Italy	May 28-June 17
9. Capital 303 E Broad St Columbus, OH 43215-3200 www.law.capital.edu	Thasos, Greece (Thessaloniki, Komotini & Samothrace)	July 9-August 5
10. Catholic Office of Institutes and Special Prgms Columbus School of Law Ste 312 CUA, Cardinal Station Washington, DC 20064 law.cua.edu	Cracow, Poland	June 17-July 29
11. Cleveland State 1801 Euclid Ave Cleveland, OH 44115 www.law.csuohio.edu	St. Petersburg, Russia	June 25-July 26
12. Cornell Cornell-Paris I Summer Institute c/o Cornell Law School Myron Taylor Hall Ithaca, NY 14853-4901 www.lawschool.cornell.edu	Paris, France	June 26-July 29
13. Detroit College 364 Law College Bldg E Lansing, MI 48824 www.dcl.edu	Cluj-Napoca, Romania	June 4-July 16
14. Detroit College	Ottawa, Canada	May 17-June 30

U.S. Law School	Location of Program	Dates
15. Drake 2507 University Ave Des Moines, IA 50311-4505 www.law.drake.edu	Nantes, France	May 29-June 23
16. Duke Box 90375 Durham, NC 27708-0375 www.law.duke.edu	Geneva, Switzerland	July 9-August 8
17. Duke	Hong Kong	July 2-August 1
18. Duquesne School of Law Duquesne University Pittsburgh, PA 15282 www.duq.edu/law	Beijing, People's Republic of China	June 5-June 23
19. Duquesne	Dublin, Ireland	June 12-July 7
20. Duquesne	Moscow, Russia	Not operating
21. Florida Student Affairs Office 164 Holland Hall Spessard L. Holland Law Ctr PO Box 117621 Gainesville, FL 32611-7621 www.law.ufl.edu/students	Cape Town, South Africa	June 12-July 28
22. Florida	Montpellier, France	June 25-July 29
23. Florida	San José, Costa Rica	June 29-July 31
24. Florida	Warsaw, Poland	Not operating
25. Florida State 425 W Jefferson St Tallahassee, FL 32306 www.law.fsu.edu	Barbados, West Indies	June 6-July 27

U.S. Law School	Location of Program	Dates
26. Florida State	Oxford, England	July 4-August 10
27. Florida State	Prague, Czech Republic	May 22-June 23
28. George Washington Office of Summer, Special, and Intl Prgms 609 22nd St. NW Washington, DC 20052 www.gwu.edu/~specprog	Oxford, England	July 9-August 5
29. Georgetown Summer Law Prgm Georgetown Univ Law Ctr 600 New Jersey Ave NW Washington, DC 20001 www.law.georgetown.edu/intl	Florence, Italy	June 4-July 3
30. Georgetown	Heidelberg, Germany	July 25-August 15
31. Georgia State GSU College of Law PO Box 4037 Atlanta, GA 30302 law.gsu.edu/students/programs	Linz, Austria	May 18-June 18
32. Golden Gate 536 Mission St San Francisco, CA 94105 www.ggu.edu/schools/law	Bangkok, Thailand	May 29-July 11
33. Golden Gate/South Texas	Istanbul, Turkey	Not operating
34. Hamline 1536 Hewitt Ave St Paul, MN 55104 www.hamline.edu/law/acadprogs	Bergen, Norway	May 21-June 10
35. Hamline	Jerusalem, Israel	July 2-July 31
36. Hamline	Modena, Italy	June 28-July 27

U.S. Law School	Location of Program	Dates
37. Hofstra 121 Hofstra University Hempstead, NY 11549 www.hofstra.edu/Academics/Law	Nice, France	July 3-July 28
38. Houston Univ of Houston Law Ctr Houston, TX 77204-6370 www.law.uh.edu	Mexico City, Mexico	May 23-June 30
39. Howard Howard University School of Law 2900 Van Ness St. NW Washington DC 20008 www.law.howard.edu	Cape Town, South Africa	June 15-July 25
40. Indiana-Bloomington	Nottingham, England	Not operating
41. Indiana-Indianapolis 735 W New York St Indianapolis, IN 46202 www.iulaw.indy.indiana.edu	Beijing, People's Republic of China	May 26-June 23
42. Indiana-Indianapolis	Lille, France	June 1-July 14
43. Iowa Melrose and Byington Iowa City, IA 52242 www.uiowa.edu/~lawcoll	Arcachon, France	May 14-June 17
44. Louisiana State LSU Law Center Rm 366 Baton Rouge, LA 70803 www.law.lsu.edu	Aix-en-Provence, France	June 12-July 22
45. Loyola-Chicago Study Law Abroad Programs One E Pearson St Chicago, IL 60611 www.luc.edu/schools/law	Oxford, England Strasbourg, France Luxembourg City, Luxembourg Brussels, Belgium	June 25-July 22
46. Loyola-Chicago	Rome, Italy	May 28-June 24

U.S. Law School	Location of Program	Dates
47. Loyola-Los Angeles 919 S. Albany St PO Box 15019 Los Angeles, CA 90015 www.lls.edu	San José, Costa Rica	July 15-August 8
48. Loyola-New Orleans 7214 St. Charles Ave New Orleans, LA 70118 www.loyno.edu/law	Cuernavaca, Mexico	May 27-July 2
49. Loyola-New Orleans	Kyoto, Japan	May 24-June 26
50. Loyola-New Orleans	San José, Costa Rica	July 2-July 16
51. Loyola-New Orleans	Vienna, Austria	July 3-July 29
52. Loyola-New Orleans/Touro	Moscow, Russia Budapest, Hungary	May 24-June 17
53. McGeorge 3200 Fifth Ave Sacramento, CA 95817 www.mcgeorge.edu	Salzburg, Austria	July 8-July 29
54. Marquette PO Box 1881 Milwaukee, WI 53201 www.marquette.edu/law	Queensland, Australia	June 25-July 23
55. Miami Coral Gables, FL 33124-0221 www.law.miami.edu	Barcelona, Fuengirola/Malaga, Madrid, Spain	June 12-August 3
56. Miami	London, England	June 19-August 6
57. Mississippi University, MS 38677 www.olemiss.edu/depts/ law_school	Cambridge, England	July 2-August 10

U.S. Law School	Location of Program	Dates
58. Missouri-Kansas City 5100 Rockhill Rd Kansas City, MO 64110 www.law.umkc.edu	Beijing, People's Republic of China	May 21-June 11
59. Missouri-Kansas City	Dublin, Ireland	June 12-July 24
60. New Mexico/Southeastern/ Texas Tech 1117 Stanford NE Albuquerque, NM 87107 lawschool.unm.edu	Guanajuato, Mexico	June 18-July 22
61. North Carolina Van Hecke-Wettach Hall 100 Ridge Rd CB #3380 Chapel Hill, NC 27599 www.law.unc.edu	Sydney, Australia	June 4-July 5
62. Northern Illinois Swen Parson Hall, Rm 276 DeKalb, IL 60115 www.niu.edu/claw	Agen, France	June 8-July 15
63. Notre Dame Notre Dame, IN 46556 www.nd.edu/~ndlaw	London, England	July 3-August 9
64. Nova Southeastern 3305 College Ave Ft Lauderdale, FL 33314 www.nsulaw.nova.edu	Cambridge, England	June 18-August 10
65. Nova Southeastern	Caracas, Venezuela	July 2-August 6
66. Nova Southeastern	San José, Costa Rica	May 29-July 2
67. Nova Southeastern/American	Haifa, Israel	May 28-June 29

U.S. Law School	Location of Program	Dates
68. Ohio State Drinko Hall 55 W 12th Ave Columbus, OH 43210 www.osu.edu/units/law	Oxford, England	July 5-August 8
69. Oklahoma Oxford Summer Prgm 300 W. Timberdell Rd Norman, OK 73019 www.law.ou.edu/ admissions/oxford	Oxford, England	July 2-August 5
70. Pennsylvania State Dickinson School of Law 150 S College St Carlisle, PA 17013 www.dsl.edu	Florence, Italy	May 29-June 23
71. Pennsylvania State	Strasbourg, France Vienna, Austria	June 24-July 26
72. Pepperdine Overseas Prgms, School of Law Malibu, CA 90263 law.pepperdine.edu	London, England	May 29-July 7
73. Pontificia Universidad Católica de Puerto Rico 2250 Avenida Las Américas Ste 543 Ponce, PR 00717 www.pucpr.edu/derecho	Toledo, Spain	May 26-June 26
74. Puerto Rico PO Box 23349 San Juan, PR 00931-3349 www.rrp.upr.edu/derecho.htm	Barcelona, Spain	June 2-August 6
75. Quinnipiac 275 Mt Carmel Ave Hamden, CT 06518 law.quinnipiac.edu	Dublin, Ireland	June 12-July 18

U.S. Law School	Location of Program	Dates
76. Regent 1000 University Dr Virginia Beach, VA 23464 www.regent.edu/acad/schlaw	Strasbourg, France	June 28-August 3
77. Richmond TC Williams School of Law Richmond, VA 23173 law.richmond.edu	Cambridge, England	July 9-August 12
78. Roger Williams 10 Metacom Ave Bristol, RI 02809 www.rwu.edu/law	Lisbon, Portugal	July 10-July 31
79. Roger Williams	London, England	June 19-July 7
80. Samford 800 Lakeshore Dr Birmingham, AL 35229 www.samford.edu/schools/law	Victoria, British Columbia	July 3-July 31
81. Samford/South Texas	Durham, England	July 2-August 2
82. Samford/South Texas	São Paulo, Brazil	Not operating
83. San Diego 5998 Alcala Park San Diego, CA 92110 www.acusd.edu/usdlaw	Barcelona, Spain	May 29-June 23
84. San Diego	Dublin, Ireland	July 3-August 4
85. San Diego	Florence, Italy	May 29-June 23
86. San Diego	London, England	July 5-August 5
87. San Diego	Moscow, Russia	May 28-August 4
88. San Diego	Oxford, England	July 4-August 4

U.S. Law School	Location of Program	Dates
89. San Diego	Paris, France	July 3-August 4
90. San Francisco 2130 Fulton St San Francisco, CA 94117 www.usfca.edu/law	Bali, Indonesia	June 18-July 8
91. San Francisco	Dublin, Ireland	June 11-July 1
92. San Francisco	Prague, Czech Republic	June 17-July 31
93. Santa Clara 500 El Camino Real Santa Clara, CA 95053 www.scu.edu/law	Budapest, Hungary	June 5-July 21
94. Santa Clara	Geneva, Switzerland Strasbourg, France	June 10-July 28
95. Santa Clara	Hong Kong Beijing, People's Republic of China	June 8-August 1
96. Santa Clara	Munich, Germany	June 12-July 28
97. Santa Clara	Oxford, England	July 2-August 11
98. Santa Clara	Seoul, South Korea	June 4-July 21
99. Santa Clara	Singapore Kuala Lumpur, Malaysia Bangkok, Thailand Ho Chi Minh City, Vietnam	June 5-July 21
100. Santa Clara	Tokyo, Japan	June 5-July 21
101. Seton Hall One Newark Ctr Newark, NJ 07102 law.shu.edu	Cairo, Egypt	June 4-July 15

U.S. Law School	Location of Program	Dates
102. Seton Hall	Milan, Parma, & Genoa, Italy	June 11-July 14
103. South Texas/California Western/William Mitchell/ New England South Texas College of Law 1303 San Jacinto Houston, TX 77002 www.stcl.edu	Valletta, Malta	May 27-June 23
104. Southern Methodist Hillcrest & Daniel Dallas, TX 75275 www.law.smu.edu	Oxford, England	July 4-August 12
105. Southwestern 675 S Westmoreland Ave Los Angeles, CA 90005 www.swlaw.edu	Buenos Aires, Argentina	May 29-July 1
106. Southwestern	Vancouver, BC, Canada	May 29-June 27
107. St. Mary's One Camino Santa Maria San Antonio, TX 78228 204.158.207.3	Innsbruck, Austria	July 2-August 5
108. St. Thomas 16400 NW 32nd Ave Miami, FL 33054 www.stu.edu/lawschool	El Escorial, Spain	May 27-June 27
109. Stetson 1401 61st St S St Petersburg, FL 33707 www.law.stetson.edu/international	Tallinn, Estonia	July 17-August 11
110. Suffolk 41 Temple St, Beacon Hill Boston, MA 02114 www.law.suffolk.edu	Lund, Sweden	June 18-July 11

U.S. Law School	Location of Program	Dates
111. Syracuse Summer Programs College of Law, Ste 340 Syracuse, NY 13244 www.law.syr.edu	Harare, Zimbabwe	May 16-August 4
112. Syracuse	Kowloon, Hong Kong	Not operating
113. Syracuse	London, England	May 30-July 21
114. Temple 1719 N Broad St Philadelphia, PA 19122 www2.law.temple.edu	Athens, Greece	June 3-July 7
115. Temple	Rome, Italy	June 9-July 18
116. Temple	Tel Aviv, Israel	May 29-July 10
117. Thomas M. Cooley 217 S Capitol Ave PO Box 13038 Lansing, MI 48901 www.cooleylaw.edu	Toronto, Canada	May 20-July 1
118. Touro 300 Nassau Rd Huntington, NY 11743 www.tourolaw.edu	Moscow, Russia	May 24-June 17
119. Touro	Xiamen, China	May 29-June 30
120. Touro/South Texas	Shimla, India	May 29-July 3
121. Tulane John Giffen Weinmann Hall 6329 Freret St New Orleans, LA 70118 www.law.tulane.edu	Amsterdam, The Netherlands	July 3-August 12
122. Tulane	Berlin, Germany	July 31-August 12

U.S. Law School	Location of Program	Dates
123. Tulane	Cambridge, England	July 3-July 29
124. Tulane	Paris, France	July 3-July 31
125. Tulane	Rhodes, Greece	May 28-June 16
126. Tulane	Siena, Italy	June 5-July 8
127. Tulane	Spetses, Greece	June 18-July 7
128. Tulane	Thessaloniki, Greece	July 9-July 28
129. Tulane/Albany	Montreal, Quebec, Canada	July 2-August 10
130. Tulane/Yeshiva	Jerusalem, Israel	July 16-August 10
131. Tulsa 3120 E 4th Pl Tulsa, OK 74104 www.utulsa.edu/law	Buenos Aires, Argentina	July 17-August 14
132. Tulsa	Dublin, Ireland	June 14-July 13
133. Valparaiso Wesemann Hall 656 S Greenwich St Valparaiso, IN 46383 www.valpo.edu/law	Cambridge/ London, England	July 2-August 8
134. Wake Forest Worrell Professional Ctr for Law & Mgmt, Rm 2312 Winston-Salem, NC 27109 www.law.wfu.edu	London, England	May 31-June 27
135. Wake Forest	Venice, Italy	July 3-July 27
136. Washburn 1700 College Topeka, KS 66621 washburnlaw.edu	London, England	June 20-July 26

U.S. Law School	Location of Program	Dates
137. Widener 4601 Concord Pike PO Box 7474 Wilmington, DE 19803 www.law.widener.edu	Geneva, Switzerland	June 15-July 23
138. Widener	Nairobi, Kenya	June 12-July 25
139. Widener	Sydney, Australia	June 16-July 21
140. William & Mary S Henry St PO Box 8795 Williamsburg, VA 23187 warthog.cc.wm.edu/law	Madrid, Spain	July 2-August 2
141. William Mitchell/California Western/New England/ South Texas William Mitchell College of Law 875 Summit Ave St Paul, MN 55105 www.wmitchell.edu	London, England	June 25-July 28
142. Willamette 245 Winter St SE Salem, OR 97301 www.willamette.edu/wucl	Shanghai, China	June 19-July 16
143. Yeshiva 55 Fifth Ave New York, NY 10003 www.cardozo.yu.edu	Budapest, Hungary	July 10-August 4

Appendix B
Nongovernmental Organizations Dealing with International Issues in Washington, D.C.

Africa-America Institute. 1625 Massachusetts Ave. NW, Suite 400, Washington, D.C. 20036, <www.aaionline.org>. A nonprofit organization that expands education and professional training opportunities for Africans, fosters greater understanding of Africa in America, and promotes mutually beneficial U.S.-Africa relations.

Africare. 440 R St. NW, Washington, D.C. 20001, <www.africare.org>. Nonprofit organization that works to improve the quality of life in rural Africa.

American Security Council. 1155 15th St. NW, Suite 712, Washington, D.C. 20005.

American Society of International Law. 2223 Massachusetts Ave. NW, Washington, D.C. 20008, <www.asil.org>.

Amnesty International USA. 304 Pennsylvania Ave. SE, Washington, D.C. 20003, <www.amnesty.org>. A nonprofit organization that works to protect human rights worldwide.

Arms Control Association. 1726 M St. NW, Suite 201, Washington, D.C. 20036, <www.armscontrol.org>. National nonpartisan membership organization that promotes public understanding of and support for effective arms control policies.

Asia Foundation. 1779 Massachusetts Ave. NW, Suite 815, Washington, D.C. 20036, <www.asiafoundation.org>. A private, nonprofit, nongovernmental organization working to advance the mutual interests of the United States and the Asia-Pacific region.

Caribbean/Latin-American Action. 1818 N St. NW, Suite 500, Washington, D.C. 20036, <www.claa.org>. A private, independent organization promoting private sector–generated economic development primarily in the countries of the Caribbean Basin.

Carnegie Endowment for International Peace. 1779 Massachusetts Ave. NW, Washington, D.C. 20036, <www.ceip.org>. A private nonprofit organization dedicated to advancing cooperation among nations and promoting active international engagement by the United States.

Friends of the Earth. 1025 Vermont Ave. NW, Suite 300, Washington, D.C. 20005, <www.foe.org>. Nonprofit organization dedicated to environmental, biological, and cultural preservation.

Greenpeace, USA. 702 H Street NW, Washington, D.C. 20001, <www.greenpeaceusa.org>. Works to protect the global environment.

National Council for World Affairs. 1726 M St. NW, Suite 800, Washington, D.C. 20036.

National Foreign Trade Council. 1625 K St. NW, Suite 1090, Washington, D.C. 20006. Trade association that deals with U.S. public policy affecting international trade and investment.

United Nations Association of the United States of America. 1779 Massachusetts Ave. NW, Suite 610, Washington, D.C. 20036, <www.unausa.org>. A nonprofit, nonpartisan national organization working to enhance U.S. participation in the United Nations.

World Wildlife Fund, 1250 24th St. NW, Suite 500, Washington, D.C. 20036, <www.worldwildlife.org>. Privately supported organization dedicated to protecting the world's wildlife and wildlands.

Appendix C
Internet Resources

These Web sites are only a starting point in your pursuit of an international legal career.

FEDERAL GOVERNMENT–RELATED WEB SITES

www.usda.gov Department of Agriculture.
www.ogc.doc.gov Department of Commerce.
www.doe.gov Department of Energy.
www.usdoj.gov Department of Justice.
www.dol.gov Department of Labor.
www.state.gov/www/careers Department of State.
www.treas.gov/jobs Department of the Treasury.
www.epa.gov Environmental Protection Agency.
www.exim.gov Export-Import Bank of the United States.
www.fcc.gov/jobs Federal Communications Commission.
www.ftc.gov Federal Trade Commission.
www.fda.gov Food & Drug Administration.
www.ins.org Immigration and Naturalization Service.
www.nasa.org National Aeronautics & Space Administration.
www.uspto.gov Patent & Trademark Office.
www.ustr.gov/about-ustr/employment.shtml Office of the U.S. Trade Representative.
www.opic.gov Overseas Private Investment Corporation (OPIC).
www.sec.gov Securities & Exchange Commission.
www.usaid.gov U.S. Agency for International Development.
www.uscit.gov U.S. Court of International Trade.
www.usitc.gov U.S. International Trade Commission.

INTERNATIONAL WEB SITES

www.interaction.org/jobs Web site of the American Council for Voluntary International Action lists job resources, internship and volunteer opportunities, and position openings (by subscription) in international development organizations.

www.aals.org Association of American Law Schools; provides information on law faculty positions.

www.accessjobs.org ACCESS: Networking in the Public Interest is a resource for employment, internships, and career development for nonprofit organizations worldwide.

www.ecojobs.com Environmental career opportunities.

www.ipcenter.com Intellectual Property Center; includes job listings.

www.iadb.org Inter-American Development Bank.

www.icclaw.com International Center for Commercial Law.

www.icnl.org International Center for Not-for-Profit Law.

www.icrc.org International Committee of the Red Cross.

www.ifc.org International Finance Corporation.

www.humanrights@hrlawgroup.org International Human Rights Law Group.

www.ilo.org International Labour Organization; has Young Professionals and internship programs.

www.lawgazette.co.uk A publication of the Law Society of England and Wales that features online job searches.

www.lawsoc.org.uk Law Society of England and Wales (lists positions available at the Law Society).

www.recruitment.lawsociety.org.uk Legal recruitment agency sponsored by the Law Society of England and Wales.

www.oas.org Organization of American States.

www.owit.org Organization of Women in International Trade; can browse a list of current job openings but need subscription for full descriptions.

www.pslawnet.org The Public Service Law Network Worldwide (PSLawNet) is a global network of some 120 member law schools and nearly 10,000 law-related public service organizations and offices around the world. To that end, PSLawNet offers information on a broad range of pro bono and public service opportunities.

www.rightsinternational.org Web site for the Center for Human Rights Law includes information on internship and other programs.

http://www.un.org/Depts/OHRM/index.html Employment Web site of the United Nations.

www.worldbank.org The World Bank.

www.iucn.org The World Conservation Union.

www.wipo.org World Intellectual Property Organization.

www.wto.org World Trade Organization.

LEGAL CAREER WEB SITES

www.acca.com/jobline/index.html Interactive employment service of the American Corporate Counsel Association.

www.attorneyjobs.com Lists attorney jobs in the United States and abroad.

www.emplawyernet.com

www.hg.org

www.JDPost.com Web site operated by law students; includes large job board.

www.job-hunt.org/law.shtml

jobs.lawinfo.com

www.lawbulletin.com Publishers of the *Chicago Daily Law Bulletin*; can search job ads online.

www.lawjobs.com

legalemploy.com Provides links to legal-related employment.

Index

A

The ABA Guide to International Business Negotiations, 85

Academic international law, 169–76
  accelerating pace of, 175
  communication in, 175
  employment opportunities in, 173–74
  improvements in international legal education, 171–72
  improvements in pre-legal international education, 170–71
  reseach developments, 174
  ubiquity of the international LL.M degree, 172–73

Accounting, international law practice and, 51

Admiralty practice, 137–41
  advantages, 139–40
  disadvantages, 138–39
  starting out, 140–41
  training for, 140

Africa-America Institute, 191

Africare, 191

Agency for International Development, U.S. (USAID), 110

Agriculture, U.S. Department of, 109–10

American Arbitration Association (AAA), 55
  Corporate Counsel Committee, 58

American Bar Association (ABA)
  approved foreign summer programs, 2000, 177–90
  International Lawyer's Deskbook, 28
  Section of International Law and Practice, 58, 65, 160, 170
  number of members in, 169
  Section on Legal Education and Admission to, 9–10

American Corporate Counsel Association, 88

American Review of International Arbitration, 65

American Security Council, 191

American Society of International Law, 58, 160, 170

Amnesty International USA, 160, 191

Anti-Boycott and Export Administration Regulations, 37

Anti-bribery statutes, 40

Arbitration. *See* International commercial arbitration

Arbitration International, 65

Arms Control Association, 191

Arthur Young & Company, 95

Asia Foundation, 192

B

Baker & McKenzie, 13

Basel Convention on the Control of Transboundary Movements of Hazardous Wastes and Their Disposal, 120

Boutique firm, 67
  international, 24

C

Career preparation, 85–88
  for admiralty law, 140
  for international commercial arbitration, 63–66

V

WXYZ